Million Dollar Kick

God is Good!

Dan Kaler

xulon PRESS

Contents

Acknowledgements

First and foremost, I would like to thank my Heavenly Father for the gift of life and the countless blessings that I have experienced in my journey. May this book be used for His glory.

Next, I would like to thank my earthly parents. Dad, thank you for instilling a belief in God and sharing all those moments playing sports in our backyard. Mom, thank you for introducing me to Jesus and consistently displaying your loving tenderness.

To my family. Kathy, I love you and am so thankful that God has placed us together. Your loving spirit is a daily reminder of God's goodness. Jacob and Andrew, this book was intended for you – may you continue your spiritual growth and experience God's goodness all the days of your life.

To those who contributed to the final manuscript. Coach Bowden, your example of leadership and perseverance is a testament for all people to follow.

To my field goal kicking mentors; John Carney, Rian Lindell, and Greg Stoller. It was my pleasure to learn from you — may your post season be filled with God's blessings.

To those who helped review my manuscript. A "graceful" thank you to my church family; Pastor Dave, Randy, Dean, Kristen and Vicki. A "geographical" thank you to my friends at work; Matt and Tom. A "green and gold" thank you to the Packer organization; Bob Harlan and Wayne Larrivee.

Finally, I would also like to recognize the musical talents of Casting Crowns, Chris Tomlin, Jeremy Camp, and Steven Curtis Chapman, which served to provide inspiration while typing my manuscript. May God continue to bless your music ministry.

Introduction – The Ultimate Goal

Athletic accomplishment is the ultimate goal for the professional athlete, the amateur athlete or even the weekend warrior. When athletic accomplishment is coupled with monetary reward, then the desire to reach the ultimate goal is even more attractive. However, the sensation of reaching the ultimate goal can be a short-lived experience.

For me, the key issue was finally realizing that I have been offered a sustaining joy that is far greater than any athletic accomplishment or monetary prize. It took some time to change my perspective. But through my Hershey Million Dollar Kick experience, I realized that God is more concerned about my spiritual growth than my financial growth. And looking back on my million dollar journey, I have a deeper appreciation for the events that have occurred in my life, the people placed in my life, and the simple joy of receiving God's blessings.

Initially, my idea was to write a book that I could pass on to my sons or share with some close friends. But while recounting my journey in this book, I realized that a broader audience could benefit from this message. Thus, it is my desire that this book may help you to arrive at the same conclusion: that through all of life's mountain top and valley experiences there is one reliable, dependable truth – God is good!

CHAPTER 1

Memories

A s a child, I would often dream of being a professional athlete, making the game winning play, hearing the applause of the crowded stadium, and celebrating with my teammates. And later as an adult, I was granted a chance to live out that dream – the Hershey Million Dollar Kick.

Some Miracle Kicks

When I was about 10 years old, I recall my father telling the story of Tom Dempsey's record-breaking field goal kick. This was the story of a guy who was born with a deformed right foot, but he did not let this limit his athletic potential. In fact, Tom Dempsey eventually became a kicker in the National Football League and still is recognized for kicking a record-setting 63 yard field goal.[1]

As I look back, I think my father intended to tell the Tom Dempsey story as a motivational talk on "doing the best with what God gave you." But I gained a lot more. Specifically, this was living proof of a "David versus Goliath" story of accomplishment regardless of the perceived limitations.

Another favorite childhood memory was a blocked field goal turned into a touchdown for the Green Bay Packers. This goes back to the days when the Packers were starving for a victory. And for a Packer fan living in northern Illinois, I was surrounded by Bear fans. A win over the Bears would provide bragging rights at school that following Monday morning.

It was the first game of the 1980 season; the Green Bay Packers would host the rival Chicago Bears. The game was a tough defensive battle with each team collecting only 2 field goals during regulation time. So with the score tied 6 - 6 in overtime, the Packers field goal kicker, Chester Marcol, lined up for a fairly easy kick. And then as the football was kicked onward, I heard an unexpected sound of a blocked kick (similar to the deflating "thump" from a tire running over a spike). I lost track of the ball for a moment, and then, all of sudden I saw Chester Marcol running around the corner hugging the ball like a bag of groceries and crossing into the end zone for a touchdown. It was not pretty, but it was a glorious day for Packer fans living in Bear country!

For those watching on television, there was an added and unexpected dash of humor. Veteran announcer Lindsey Nelson, calling the play-by-play for CBS, was so overcome ... that all he could do was keep repeating the kicker's name. Temporarily unable to describe what had just happened, he kept exclaiming "Chester Marcol! Chester Marcol! Chester Marcol!" without ever describing what had just happened in the game."[2]

And then there was that windy day in Laramie, Wyoming. It was sometime in October during my senior year of college at the University of Wyoming. Although I was pursuing a degree in civil engineering, my main interest was playing intramural sports. So after a full day of attending classes, one of my college roommates and I went to a local football field for a simulated punt, pass and kick competition. After briefly throwing the football to one another, we quickly realized that the gusting winds would substantially improve the flight of the football. When it came time to kick field goals, we decided to have the wind at our backs. And instead of using a kicking tee, we decided that the holder would place the football on their foot and then elevate their foot to provide a better launch angle. With these ideal conditions for our contest, I was able to make a 55 yard field goal that day! If only a kicker could have the wind at their back on every kick – or maybe for just one special kick.

Nothing Like a Day at the Old Ball Park!

For some reason, many of my favorite life experiences have occurred on the athletic field. Take for example, the Cubs game at Wrigley Field on June 20, 1987. Ah yes, I remember it well – three of my long time friends from high school and I were sitting in the outfield bleachers on a sunny Saturday afternoon.

My friends and I arrived at the game a couple hours early, and consequently, we were able to pick out the location of our seats. Since the bleacher tickets were classified as general admission, we were able to sit anywhere in the bleacher section. Our choice was always front row as close to center field as possible (not bad, for a $4 ticket).

The Cubs were hosting the Pittsburgh Pirates, and there was a young player named Barry Bonds playing for the Pirates that day. At that time, all I knew about Barry Bonds was that his dad was a famous baseball player. This was Barry's second year in Major League Baseball and he had not yet displayed his potential as a home run hitter. In fact, he was the lead off hitter for the Pirates that day.[3]

When Barry stepped in the batter's box to lead off the game, the stadium was filled with optimistic Cub fans – after all, the opponent had not scored yet. But those feelings would soon change with the very first batter.

The Cub's pitcher that day, Greg Maddux, was another young player who had yet to establish his name in Major League Baseball. Looking back at it now, this game was an early battle for two future hall of fame players. I don't recall how many pitches were thrown to Barry, but Greg eventually delivered a pitch that Barry blasted toward center field.

Back, Back, Back ...

I saw the ball coming my way right off the bat and the ball continued to fly right at me. I quickly laid down my cigar (yes, we were celebrating even before the first pitch), then stood up and leaned over the famous ivy wall of Wrigley Field. As the Cub's outfielder sprinted toward the wall, I realized the ball would travel beyond his outstretched glove. The baseball appeared to be gaining speed and I could now tell that it would just barely clear the wall. I placed both my hands together to form a receiving pocket for the catch, and then felt a sharp sting as the ball landed into my hands.

Still in a state of amazement, I looked over at my friends and showed them the ball. I raised the ball up in the air and joyfully exchanged a series of "high fives" with my friends. Next, I heard the chant of "Throw it back, throw it back, throw it back ..." from all the diehard Cub fans in the bleachers. I looked over at my friends and asked them, "What should I do?"

"You gotta send it back," they mutually shouted.

"Well, here it goes," I replied.

And with that, I nodded at my friends and leaned back to start my overhand "return to sender" delivery. Since I had previously played centerfield in high school, I took it as a challenge to see how far I could throw it back onto the field. After I released the ball, I could hear the roar of the fans. I watched as the ball landed just in front of the infield base path and continued to roll toward the pitcher's mound. I guess I did what only a true Cub fan would do – find some sense of joy even when you're down.

And now with Barry Bonds approaching record breaking status, a home run baseball can bring a lot of money. But would money make me a better person in the eyes of God? And come to think of it, how many people can say that they actually threw back a Barry Bonds home run ball?

The Greater Purpose

Some people may call it good luck, some may call it being at the right place at the right time – but I know the events of my life are more than random chance. As I look back, I can now see with better clarity how certain events have shaped my life. And in particular, the Hershey Million Dollar Kick provided a deeper understanding

of what is really important in life.

CHAPTER 2

The Selection

There it was – the grocery store display containing the entry forms for the Hershey Million Dollar Kick. I grabbed a handful of entry forms and quickly scanned the terms of the contest. The contest was open to any legal resident over 21 years old, a limit of one contest entry per day, and all entries must be received by January 8, 2001.

The contest drawing was designed to select 4 random entries. The four contestants would compete at a qualifying event in San Diego for the chance to advance to Tampa, Florida for the Hershey Million Dollar Kick at Super Bowl XXXV. I always had the feeling that my chance would come some day – and for some reason, I felt that this was the year.

Perhaps my eternal optimism was related to being a diehard fan of Chicago Cubs and Green Bay Packers during the 1970 - 1980 era. So with a hopeful outlook, I started my field goal kicking preparations just in case my name was selected as a contestant. Usually, I would bring my two sons (age 6 and 8) to a nearby schoolyard to play soccer or football with them, and then I would attempt a few field goals. It had been a while since I had kicked a football, but I gradually regained my soccer-style form. And with the last kick of the day, I would visualize being in front of a crowded stadium to attempt the million dollar kick and feel the joy of seeing the ball split the uprights.

I often thought of receiving a phone call announcing that I was selected as one of the contestants. I even identified the timeframe that I might receive the phone call – it would occur sometime around January 8th (since that was the deadline for the contest entry forms). Looking back, I really believed that I would receive the phone call. You can call it hope, faith or the gift of knowledge, but I eventually received the phone call.

Monday January 8th – Selection Day

I remember driving to work that day and thinking this may be the day that I receive a phone call announcing my selection. But once I arrived at work, I was very busy with meetings and my earlier thoughts had temporarily left.

Over my lunch hour, I checked my voice mail – there were two messages that provided a hint of optimism. The first message was from my wife, "Dan, you are not going to believe this … please call me as soon as possible."

The next message was from Michael Seeger from SFX Events (an event promotion consulting company), and he also asked that I contact him as soon as possible. Although I did not know exactly what news my wife wanted to share, I had a pretty good feeling that I was about to receive a special surprise. And being a guy who doesn't open his presents until Christmas morning, I decided to call Michael Seeger to receive the news from the source. Upon calling Michael, I announced myself and then he responded with the statement, "Do you remember submitting a contest entry for the Hershey Million Dollar Kick?"

At that moment, I felt a great rush of excitement! Although I was always conscientious of the noise level in the office, I let my happiness exude during my conversation with Mike at that moment. I do not exactly remember my response, but I think "Wow, that's cool" would be the understatement of the year.

Mr. Seeger stated that I was selected as one of four contestants for the Hershey Million Dollar Kick. However, only one contestant would advance to the Super Bowl to attempt the Hershey Million Dollar Kick. As part of the final selection process, I would compete with three other contestants in San Diego, California next week for the chance to attempt the Hershey Million Dollar Kick at Super Bowl XXXV in Tampa, Florida.

That night, I lay in bed thinking about my selection as a contestant and trying to realize the scope of this opportunity – a chance to make one million dollars in front of a national television audience. Needless to say, I didn't sleep much that night. It was a pleasant state of sleeplessness – the anticipation of that special day!

Tuesday January 9ᵗʰ – Am I Dreaming?

When I awoke the next morning, I truly experienced the meaning of the famous motto "feeling like a million dollars." I had an overwhelming sense of excitement that did not go away. It was hard to believe, but I actually had the chance to win a million dollars! It was like a dream come true.

I needed a full day to grasp the exciting news, but now I was ready to share the exciting news with my family and friends. To get the message out quickly, I decided to send a brief e-mail message to announce my selection in the Hershey Million Dollar Kick. The following message illustrates my state of mind at that time:

Sent: Tuesday, January 09, 2001
Subject: You're not going to believe this...

THIS IS THE HONEST TO GOD TRUTH:

I was selected as a first prize winner of the Hershey's 1,000,000 kick contest. Basically, I will travel to San Diego next week to compete with four other contestants for a chance to travel to the Super Bowl & kick for a $1,000,000 prize. I was notified yesterday & hope to make arrangements to practice with a local high school coach. I am also exploring other people to help me develop my kicking skills.

I didn't sleep much last night & am quite wiped out with all this excitement. It's like a dream, but I'm still awake. Whatever the outcome, I plan to enjoy it. I just thank God for the joy & excitement!

I will try to call later to discuss all the details.

Love,
Dan

Ryan, Rian and Greg

To help transform my million dollar dream turn into reality, my first task was to contact the local high school in Camas, Washington (home of the Camas Papermakers). I wanted to determine if they had a special teams coach who might be able to provide a few tips on my kicking technique. Thankfully, I was able to meet with the Camas Special Teams Coach (Greg Stoller) who previously kicked in college for Central Washington University. Greg provided some helpful warm-up drills and evaluated my kicking style.

The next task was finding a suitable location to practice during the cold rainy weather in Washington. I called the Clark County Indoor Soccer Center in Vancouver, Washington and explained my situation to the building manager. And thankfully, he also agreed to help my quest for the million dollar kick. He offered free use of the arena during any open time slot (basically early morning on the weekend and mid-afternoon during the weekdays).

The First Ryan

My other plan of action was to seek expert advice from NFL kickers. Being a lifelong Green Bay Packer fan, my preference was to somehow meet with Ryan Longwell (the kicker for the Packers at that time). Additionally, I knew that Ryan grew up nearby in Bend, Oregon and perhaps he was back home visiting family during the off season.

By another chance circumstance, I met Ryan's mother a few years back at the Nike Outlet store in Bend Oregon. It was a Sunday afternoon and I was wearing a Packer jersey in the store. While walking down one of the aisles, I overhead a conversation about the Packer game that day. I thought it quite odd (yet very interesting) that someone in Oregon would be talking Packer football, and I decided to walk closer to their conversation.

Well, it just so happened that Ryan's high school coach was in the store and he was talking with Mrs. Longwell about Ryan's game winning field goal kick that day. Upon seeing my Packer jersey, the high school coach looked at me and stated, "Hey Packer fan, did you hear about the game today? Well, here's the mother of the player that kicked the game winning field goal."

I replied saying, "Wow, you must be very proud of your son!"

"Yes," she replied, "I got really nervous, but Ryan pulled through today."

The Packers did not play very well against the Cincinnati Bengals that day, but they were able to squeak out a victory. This was the type of game that emphasized the importance of a good field goal kicker.

I was hopeful that meeting with Ryan Longwell would improve my chances of winning the preliminary contest in San Diego. So I decided to contact the Green Bay Packers general office and explain my situation. They would not provide Ryan's phone number, but they directed me to the Special Teams Coach, Frank Novak. After explaining my situation, Mr. Novak stated that he did not know if Ryan was at home or vacationing during the off-season. However, he said that he would try to locate Ryan and perhaps Ryan might call me to discuss training options.

The Other Rian

Unfortunately, I never heard back from Ryan Longwell. However, I was presented with an opportunity to meet with another local kicker that made the ranks of the NFL. An acquaintance from my church worked with the brother of Rian Lindell (the kicker for the Seattle Seahawks at that time) and through this acquaintance, I learned that Rian was living in the Seattle area during the off season. And thankfully, I was able to obtain his phone number.

Rian Lindell attended a local high school in Vancouver, Washington, and then went on to play football for Washington State University. After kicking very well at the collegiate level, Rian was signed as a free agent with the Seahawks and made the final roster. Rian kicked very well for the Seahawks that year, including a few game winning kicks and several field goals over 50 yards.

Although Rian was interested in meeting with me, our schedules did not permit us to meet prior to the competition in San Diego.

However, Rian was agreeable to conduct a future training session if I made it as the finalist for the Hershey Million Dollar Kick.

Since I was not able to meet with either Ryan Longwell or Rian Lindell, it was up to Greg Stoller of Camas High School to help prepare me for the qualifying round. We met a couple more times at the indoor soccer center to polish my kicking style. He stressed the importance of foot position and forward body motion through the ball. He even brought his video camera and captured several still frames to help evaluate my kicking technique.

Three Steps Back, Two Steps Over

A key issue in developing my kicking technique was determining the optimal number of strides for my approach to the football. For a field goal attempt in a game situation, the kicker has to get the ball off quickly (ideally within 1.4 seconds from the time the ball is snapped, placed on the ground, and then kicked from the hold). Consequently, the traditional approach involves pacing 3 steps back and 2 steps over from the location of the field goal kick.

On the other hand, the approach distance for a kickoff (as performed at the start of each football game) typically involves several more strides to generate more momentum to strike the football. Additionally, the kickoff is made from a kicking tee which serves to elevate the football and thereby provide a better launch position for the kick (similar to using a golf tee). And since the rules for the Hershey Million Dollar Kick allowed the contestants to use a kicking tee, the ideal technique would be kickoff style (thankfully, we did not have a charging defense trying to block our kick).

So while working with Coach Stoller, I strived to incorporate a kickoff style technique. We tried doubling the amount of my approach strides by pacing 6 steps back and 4 steps over; however, we discovered that I was not as consistent in either direction or distance. Thus, we decided to focus on using the 3 steps back and 2 steps over technique.

CHAPTER 3

San Diego, Here I Come!

As part of the selection for the Hershey Million Dollar Kick, each of the four contestants would receive round trip airfare to San Diego for two people, hotel accommodations and a $1,000 cash prize. Since I already won the $1,000 cash prize, my wife and I decided that we could afford to bring our two sons with us to San Diego. Regardless of the outcome, it promised to be a memorable family trip.

Monday January 15th – Meet the Contestants

We departed the Portland airport around noon that day and arrived in San Diego late that afternoon. By the time we picked up our rental car and drove to the hotel, it was just about time to meet for the dinner reception. This was an opportunity to meet the other contestants and size up the competition.

Upon coming down to the lobby area, we were approached by representatives from Hershey Foods (Traci Gentry) and SFX Corporate Consulting (Michael Seeger). They introduced all of the contestants and then we walked to a nearby restaurant for the dinner reception.

Although I received a copy of the press release for the Hershey Million Dollar Kick contestants, I had no idea of their athletic ability. The press release only provided the following information about each contestant:

Kathleen Gallagher, 37, a United States Postal Service employee from Clearwater, Florida.

Dan Kaler, 36, a digital mapping professional from Camas, Washington.

Julie Karlen, 40, a homemaker from Littleton, Colorado.

Joe Polkowski, 34, a printing pressman from Grand Rapids, Michigan.[4]

During our walk to the restaurant, I started to envision their athletic talents. As mentioned above, there were two female contestants and another male contestant. I anticipated that Joe would be my toughest competition, but you never know until you see a person kick the football. I have seen some very talented female soccer players and was not going to underestimate any of the other contestants.

The Rules and the Reward

That evening we also reviewed the rules of the contest. They explained that each of the four contestants would compete in a field goal competition and would receive points for each successful kick. Each contestant would attempt one field goal kick from 15 yards, 25 yards, and 35 yards. The scoring system was established as follows:

Contestants will receive one (1) point for a successful kick from 15 yards, three (3) points for a successful kick from 25 yards, and five (5) points from 35 yards. If a tie occurs, the tie-breaker will take place at a 30 yard distance. Victory is earned by one contestant making their kick, and the other

contestant failing to make their attempt.[5]

The person with the most points would receive an expense paid

trip to Super Bowl XXXV in Tampa, Florida, a $10,000 cash prize,

and a chance to kick for $1,000,000. And this year, there would be

one key change for the Hershey Million Dollar Kick – the distance

of the kick would be established by a field goal kicker in the National

Football League (NFL).

The Professional Choice

The NFL kicker chosen this year was John Carney (the kicker

for the San Diego Chargers at that time). A few days prior to Super

Bowl Sunday, John would attempt kicks from 50, 55, and 60 yards

to establish the final distance for the Hershey Million Dollar Kick.

For each successful field goal, the distance for the Hershey Million

Dollar Kick would move 5 yards closer. Thus, the distance could be

as far as 40 yards if John missed all his kicks, or as close as 25 yards

if John made all three of his kicks.

I knew that John was a veteran kicker in the National Football League, but my most vivid memory was a game during his college days at the University of Notre Dame. While home from college during my Thanksgiving break, I distinctly recall watching a classic wet and muddy game in which John Carney made several key field goals that day to help lead the University of Notre Dame Irish overcome the University of Southern California Trojans. Although I knew that John was a good kicker, I was about to find out that he was also a man of integrity.

Tuesday January 16th – The Practice Day

The next day we traveled to the San Diego Charger practice facility for the training session with John Carney. I was fairly relaxed for the first day of practice, but I still wondered about my level of competition. Would I be competing against former women soccer players that could boot the football like a soccer ball? Would Joe possess a stronger leg? In only a few moments, I would know for sure.

Upon arriving at the training facility, we walked over to the practice field and we could see John Carney kicking at the far end zone. The Hershey staff suggested that we jog or stretch out while we wait for John to conclude his work out. This was our chance to watch John and measure his talents at kicking the football. We observed that John was not that tall, but he appeared to have a very solid physique. As we watched John kick, we could hear a loud "boom" sound as he struck the football and sent it flying towards goal post.

Next, John came over to introduce himself and express his desire to help us win a million dollars. He described some basic details for kicking a football and stated that he would use today to evaluate our technique for the competition tomorrow. He seemed very genuine and interested in helping all of us improve our chances in the contest. And as a statement of his kicking ability, he placed the ball in the kicking tee from 65 yards away and then calmly boomed the ball through the uprights.

Wednesday January 17th – The Contest Day

The following day we conducted the field goal contest. The rules required each contestant to draw a number to determine the order of kicking. My desire was to be selected as either the first or last contestant to attempt each field goal.

Although there would be some jitters with being the first contestant, my thoughts were to place additional pressure on the other contestants by making my initial kick. I was familiar with the golfing ritual of "having the honor" of hitting first, and was aware that hitting a nice first shot can mentally put pressure on your opponent. However, being the final contestant to kick would provide a better understanding of my circumstances in the contest. If I was leading at that point, I would be more relaxed in my attempt. Or if I was behind in the point total, I would clearly know the required outcome to regain the lead.

As it turned out, I drew the first kicking position for each round. The first attempt was from 15 yards. I felt very confident at this distance, but I also knew that it was certainly possible to be off target. I had seen the other contestants make a 15 yard kick during our training session, and I really felt that missing this attempt would put me in a deep hole. Using golf as an analogy – a 3 foot putt is easy to perform on the putting green, but there is a lot more pressure when you are competing in a tournament. At this distance, I just had to make a smooth kick on the sweet spot of the football.

The Time is Now

It was now my turn to start the competition – the local camera crews were on the practice field, there was a field judge standing behind the goal posts, and my wife was on the sideline shouting some words of encouragement. I gathered my thoughts – 3 steps back, 2 steps over, focus on the middle of the football, and make a smooth kick through the football. I cautiously approached the ball, cleanly struck the ball, and then watched the ball proceed end-over-end through the uprights. After making my attempt, it was now time for the other contestants to face the goal posts. And surprisingly, all of the other contestants missed their attempt from 15 yards. Round one was a success – I was the early leader with one point!

The next kicking distance was from 25 yards. A successful kick would be worth 3 points and a failed attempt would open the door for the other contestants. In particular, I knew that both Joe and I were very capable of making this kick. If I missed my attempt, then Joe could take the lead by making his kick. I could feel the pressure of the situation. I tried to focus on my own abilities and realize that the success of my kick was totally within my control.

At the 25 yard distance, I would typically miss if I kicked the football too low or if I approached the football too quickly. The key would be a smooth motion and to make contact on the sweet spot (just slightly below the middle of the ball). Here again, I think my golf experience proved to be a helpful athletic trait. Just like a golf shot, you have to possess the discipline and patience to watch the ball all the way through the point of contact.

So, there I stood – 25 yards away and ready for the challenge. I placed the ball on the kicking tee and looked up at the field goal posts. I visualized the path of my kick and then paced back to my starting point. I paused for a brief moment, rocking my body forward and back while collecting my thoughts. I maintained focus on the ball, stepped into the kick, and heard the familiar thump sound upon kicking the ball. And yes, it was good from 25 yards away! I recall shouting an exuberant "YEAH" as the ball sailed through the uprights from 25 yards away. It was like all my emotions were summarized with this exclamatory shout. I felt a strong sense of joy and accomplishment.

Next, it would be time for Julie, Joe and Kathleen to have their chance at 25 yards. And again, I was surprised that they all missed their kick at this distance! At this stage, I was leading the competition with 4 total points. I knew that my chances for winning looked very good; however, any of the contestants could win the event by making their kick from 35 yards.

Win or Go Home

The final round was from 35 yards and a successful kick would receive 5 points. Even though I made both my attempts from 15 and 25 yards, I knew that Joe could still win by making his attempt from 35 yards. Joe had the leg strength to carry this distance, but lately he was kicking line drives that did not have adequate height. During my prior practice sessions, I very rarely made a field goal from this distance. However, I was pumped up after making my first two kicks and ready to take a full swing at the goal post.

As I placed the ball on the tee, I realized that I had to be aggressive and try to develop maximum power for the 35 yard kick. I paced my normal steps back to my starting point, focused my eyes on the sweet spot on the ball, rocked back and forth on my feet from heel to toe, and then quickly darted towards the football. My plan was to approach the ball more quickly, and thereby develop more momentum for my kick. Although I certainly struck the ball with more force, the point of contact was more towards the front part of my shoe. The football traveled a little higher than normal and landed wide right of the goal post. All I could do now was wait and hope that the other contestants would also miss their 35 yard kick.

I found my two sons among the spectators and explained to them that we had to wait for the remaining contestants to attempt their field goals. I knew that they did not yet understand the importance of the situation and I cautioned them to remain quiet while we watched the remaining field goal attempts. My wife was still standing along the sideline and she continued to video the remaining kicks.

Next, both of the female contestants (Julie Karlen and Kathleen Gallagher) would have the opportunity to kick from 35 yards. Julie Karlen had previously injured her foot during our practice session and she continued to display pain with every subsequent kick. She courageously attempted the 35 yard field goal kick, but her kick did not have enough power to carry the distance. Julie's kick attempt was followed by Kathleen Gallagher. Although Kathleen had displayed the leg strength to make a 15 yard field goal, her attempt from 35 yards also landed short of the goal post.

And then came Joe Polkowski ... could he be the Cinderella story from Grand Rapids Michigan? I was hopeful that I would prevail as the winner, but I was aware that Joe would advance to the Super Bowl if he was successful from this distance. Joe used the "straight on" kicking style and he always seemed to get a head of steam when he approached the football. It was certainly possible that he could make a kick from 35 yards.

As I stood near the back of crowd with my two sons, I was anxious to know the outcome of Joe's kick. It was helpful to discuss the consequences of the situation to my sons. My youngest son Andrew opened the conversation with the question, "Dad, did you win?"

I responded, "Not yet, we need to wait until the remaining people try their field goal kicks."

Next, Jacob asked, "When will you know if you win?"

"Well, this is their last chance to win the contest," I replied. "If they make this kick, then they win. If they miss, then I win the contest. And that means that I will get the chance to kick for one million dollars at the Super Bowl."

Then Jacob added another question, "Can we go with you to Super Bowl?"

"We'll see buddy," I answered. "We just need to be quiet now and see if they make the kick."

Before Joe lined up his kick, I noticed him speaking with his wife and she appeared to offer words of encouragement. From this brief moment of bonding with his wife, I realized that the outcome of the contest would not just impact each contestant, but also their extended family. I wondered if my wife would be disappointed in me if I lost this contest. Or would my boys think less of me because I got beat by another person? It became very apparent that one contestant was going to be happy and the rest would experience sorrow.

As I watched Joe prepare for his kick, I noticed that he walked about 10 yards behind the ball. I knew from my own experience that you get more momentum using a longer approach distance; however, it is more difficult to kick the sweet spot of the ball. The perfect kick would require a combination of power and finesse.

As Joe began his approach towards the football, he appeared to generate a great deal of speed as he kicked the ball. The football quickly flew in the direction of the goal posts, but did not gain enough height to carry the 35 yard distance. When I saw the football land short of the goal post, I wanted to remain humble in my appearance and I tried not to show any outward signs of my excitement. I just looked over to my sons and made the statement, "Hey guys, Dad's going to the Super Bowl!"

The Post Game Show

After winning the contest, I was interviewed by several local reporters. It was quite exciting to talk to the news media. I felt just like a pro athlete conducting a post game interview. This special attention was gratifying and I really enjoyed discussing the thrill of winning the contest.

After concluding my interviews, I spoke with the Hershey's staff about the plans for the next phase of the contest. Shortly thereafter, I said goodbye to John Carney and the San Diego Charger staff. Then, I drove to the closest pay phone to share the news.

First, I called my dad. "Hey dad, I did it! I won the field goal contest, and now I'm headed to the Super Bowl!"

"Wow, that's great! I'm so happy for you Tiger."

It had been quite some time since my dad used the nickname "Tiger". For me, it symbolized a statement of pride from my father. This moment brought back fond memories from my childhood, and I was glad that this accomplishment also brought a sense of joy to my father.

Next, I called my mother, brother and sister at their places of work. And then, we called Kathy's family to share the exciting news.

The TV Highlights

Before our plane left that evening, I thought it would be cool to watch the local television news report of the Hershey Million Dollar Kick competition that occurred that day. Since we had already checked out of our hotel, I decided to search for an electronics store that had an assortment of televisions. After driving by several commercial shopping areas, we found a Best Buy store shortly after 6:00 PM (hopefully, the sports segment had not aired yet). I told the family to follow my lead as we scrambled down the aisle toward the television section. I quickly found a sales associate and inquired about the local television stations. While waiting for him to change the channels on several televisions, my wife was telling the sales associate about our exciting day. I was hoping for a low key situation, but the sales associate eagerly spread the word to his colleagues. My desire for a private screening of the interviews soon became a viewing party of several sales associates and customers. It was certainly cool to see contest highlights in the store. And although we didn't buy anything, I think we provided the store with some excitement that day.

CHAPTER 4

Back Home Again

Thursday January 18th – I'm going to the Super Bowl

Upon arriving home, one of my first tasks was to change the greeting on our answering machine. The new message began with the same monotone greeting and then burst into a loud shout of excitement. The greeting now had the announcement, "Hi, this is Dan. I'm not here right now … BECAUSE I'M GOING TO THE SUPER BOWL!" It was just my way of adding a little humor to the exciting news.

Not the normal greeting at work

Before we left San Diego, I also called my boss to share the news of my advancement as the finalist for the Hershey Million Dollar Kick. I reassured him that I would return to the office Thursday;

however, I would need some more time off for the Super Bowl appearance. Apparently, he spread the news of my accomplishment with the rest of the office staff. And upon arriving at the office the next day, I was greeted with applause from the whole office staff (about 70 people). It was a very nice greeting and a special moment with my co-workers.

Later that day, I sent the following e-mail to a few close friends from my high school and college days:

Sent: Thursday, January 18, 2001 7:52 PM
Subject: It's good!

The dream continues ... I'm going to the Super Bowl! I'm waiting to wake up & realize that it's just a dream, but I guess it's really happening. I continue to thank God for the joy & excitement!

We flew to San Diego on Monday & then on Tuesday we had a training session with John Carney (the Chargers kicker). At the competition on Wednesday, I made the field goals from 15 & 25 yards. I was wide right on the 35 yard attempt, but the other contestants also missed at both 35 and 25 yards.

By winning this field goal contest, I will advance to the Super Bowl to have a chance to win $1,000,000. I tell ya it's crazy – whatever happens I'm just gonna have fun & thank God for the journey.

We will be flying to Tampa on Wednesday & I'll be attending a variety of promotional events. One event is a visit to a local children's hospital with John. I've been impressed with the class of Hershey Foods & have really enjoyed meeting John Carney – he's a real nice guy.

Well, so much for now. Thanks for all your words of encouragement. I'll be kicking live on CBS during the pre-game festivities. Whatever the outcome, I know that I already have the greatest prize – God's love for us all!

Friday January 19th – Interview with the Columbian Newspaper

After returning from San Diego, I received a request for an interview with the local newspaper (The Columbian). I spoke with their local news reporter (Mike Bailey) to summarize my selection and preparation for the Hershey Million Dollar Kick.

When asked about future plans if I won the million dollar prize, I replied that my wife and I were content with our lifestyle. We did not plan any extravagant purchases for ourselves and we viewed the contest prize as an opportunity to help others. I provided the following strategy for our spending, "If I do win the grand prize, then it will give us a chance to give more to others. Our church is planning a major expansion, and we could help with that. And we've always given to non-profit organizations, so we could do more there."[6] When pressed for an answer about splurging on ourselves, I offered that I would like to purchase an anniversary ring for Kathy and perhaps some new golf clubs for myself.

The newspaper also sent a photographer to take pictures of my training at the Clark County Indoor Soccer Center. The photographer stated that the interview and picture would be published in the Sunday paper. Needless to say, I went to the local grocery store early Sunday morning to get my copy and read the scoop on that "Million Dollar Kicker from Camas."

For me, seeing my picture in the newspaper was a special way of recognizing someone as an "important" person. I recall the time when I was playing youth football, probably about 12 years old, and the local newspaper (The Rockford Register Star) published an action picture of me running with the football. I felt just like an NFL player – several of my neighbors and classmates noticed my picture and acknowledged this "front page" day in my childhood.

As I look back on how "special" I felt about seeing my picture in the paper, I realize that receiving recognition from other people is certainly nice, but it is a short-lived feeling. I now have greater awareness that we are "loved beyond measure" in the eyes of God – regardless of whether we are a pro athlete or just an average guy who likes to kick field goals.

Training at the Indoor Soccer Center

Upon returning home from San Diego, I altered my work schedule to practice kicking at the Clark County Indoor Soccer Center from 3:00 - 3:45 PM during the week. With the cold and rainy weather conditions, this was an ideal practice environment. Additionally, it was helpful to gain experience kicking on artificial turf since the Hershey Million Dollar Kick would occur on a similar field.

Radio Interview with the "Morning Jocks"

The morning after we returned from San Diego, the phone rang about 4:30 AM – it was a morning radio show from New York. Apparently, they saw the Hershey's press release and found our number by searching listed telephone information (by the way, we have since changed to an unlisted phone number). Anyways, I agreed to talk with their host and explain my chance for a million dollars.

About 15 minutes later, I received a phone call from another east coast radio station. The common question from these interviews asked, "So what are you going to do with a million dollars?" My standard reply was that we plan to share our gift with others. Specifically, we planned to contribute to our parent's retirement, our church expansion, and our children's college savings plan. I got a little annoyed with their perception that I would be a selfish winner. In particular, I recall a radio tag team consisting of an obnoxious male host and a rude female host:

> **Obnoxious Guy**: "Ah come on … you're gonna spend it on yourself."

> **Rude Gal**: "Yeah, you'll forget about everybody once you get the money."

> **My reply**: "No, that's not my plan. I'll thank God for the opportunity regardless of the outcome. And if I make the kick, then I will share this gift with others!"

Sunday January 21st

During our church service the following Sunday, I was asked by our pastor to come forward and share my experience with the congregation. I gave a brief explanation of my selection in the contest, the competition in San Diego, and my chance to make a $1,000,000 kick at the Super Bowl. I shared my thoughts about participating in this exciting event and emphasized that my journey was a blessing from God. And regardless of the outcome, I wanted to conduct myself in a manner that would be pleasing to God.

Monday January 22nd – Encouragement at work

At the office, my co-workers continued to offer their support and encouragement. Each day I would receive a variety of upbeat greetings to express their interest in my million dollar quest. One of the county judges sent me an encouraging e-mail:

Sent: Monday, January 22, 2001 12:06 PM
To: Kaler, Dan
Subject: Good Luck!

As a former coach for both State and National Hershey's champions in Track and Field, I wanted to also give you some advice. Listen to your coaches!

Actually trying to visualize yourself out there with the big crowd and visualize yourself doing all the motions including watching it go through the uprights is probably something you have already been told. If not, it's a common coaching technique.

Looks like you have a good chance. I'll be watching and rooting for you!

Although I never wanted to be the center of attention, I really appreciated the emotional support from my co-workers.

Tuesday January 23rd – Kicking with Rian

After returning from San Diego, I contacted Rian Lindell to inquire about a tutoring session. Rian mentioned that he had scaled back his kicking during the off season; however, he would occasionally practice at the University of Washington football stadium. Although I only had a few days before flying to Tampa, we agreed that Tuesday January 23rd would work for both of us.

I recall driving to Seattle on Tuesday morning with one burning question on my mind – what if I can't develop stronger leg strength by Super Bowl Sunday? I was hopeful that Rian could identify something in my technique that would make the difference. After trying several techniques during my practice sessions (and even analyzing myself on video), I was at a loss for what to do next.

It was about a 3 hour drive to the University of Washington stadium. When I arrived in the parking lot, I searched for the employee parking area that Rian had suggested as our meeting place. As I drove closer, I noticed a guy looking in his trunk and pulling out a bag of footballs. Although we had never met, I was fairly confident that I found the right guy. As I approached him, I cautiously said, "You must be Rian."

"Hi Dan. You find the stadium okay?"

"Yeah, I could see it from the highway and your directions worked fine. Thanks again for setting up the practice session today."

As we walked over to the stadium, I quickly realized that Rian was a big guy – probably about 6' 3" and 220 pounds. He stated that he was enjoying the off season and that it was a much-needed break from the mental stress of a professional field goal kicker. I realized that this time of year was his vacation time, and I sure appreciated his willingness to spend time with me.

It was a nice morning for kicking field goals (a clear sunny day in January is not too common in Washington). As we entered the stadium, I wondered what it would feel like on game day – to hear the roar of the crowd, to feel the forceful contact with your opponent, and to experience the joy of making a key play in the game. It was a great day to be at Husky Stadium.

The bag of footballs that Rian provided were official NFL footballs designated for kicking in an NFL game. At first I was eager to use these footballs, but that would quickly change with my first field goal attempt. I started out from the 20 yard distance, and after striking the ball, I immediately discovered that these footballs were "hard as a rock." Unlike the average football, these footballs appeared to have a different type of leather and were inflated to a greater pressure. After cringing in pain for a brief moment, I asked Rian, "So why are these footballs so hard?"

"Yeah, they are fully inflated, but they also travel farther," replied Rian. "Actually, I think the equipment manager may have over-inflated these balls. But, I prefer kicking a harder football."

From that point, I knew that he was out of my league. Not only could he endure the pain of kicking a "coconut" football, but he was booming the ball like cannon fire. I decided to bow out of the "toughest foot" contest and decided to stick with kicking my softer football.

After observing some of my kicks, Rian offered a few suggestions to improve my leg strength. He stated that I appeared to have good leg whip, but I needed to lock my ankle at the time of impact. Additionally, we worked on taking more strides in my approach to the ball. This technique improved my kicking distance; however, my accuracy was still inconsistent. Overall, I was glad to have worked out with Rian Lindell, but I knew that I still would have difficulty making a field goal greater than 30 yards.

CHAPTER 5

Tampa, Here I Come!

W e really enjoyed having the boys with us in San Diego for the preliminary competition, and we gave serious thought to having them join us in Tampa. The key questions were whether we could afford the additional airfare, as well as whether the boys could handle attending all the media events leading up to the Hershey Million Dollar Kick.

As part of winning the preliminary competition, Hershey would provide round trip airfare to Tampa for two people (naturally, I chose my wife as my travel companion). Additionally, there would be several media events and promotional appearances prior to Super Bowl Sunday. The Hershey staff cautioned that having the boys along might be taxing on us, and that it may be beneficial to have another adult supervise the boys. This was a job for Grandma!

Grandma to the Rescue

Since Kathy's mother (Barbara) had the most flexible work schedule, we contacted her to determine her availability to help with watching our boys. Since Grandma Barbara lived in Illinois, we proposed a couple travel options from the Chicago airport; (a) flying direct to Tampa and join us for the Super Bowl, or (b) flying to Portland and stay at our house with the boys. Grandma Barbara said that she would submit her leave request with her employer and then let us know as soon as possible. In the mean time, I checked on airfare costs for all the flight options; Chicago to Portland, Chicago to Tampa, and as well as Portland to Tampa.

As it turned out, it would be very expensive to purchase a flight from Portland to Tampa with less than 14 days notice (somewhere around $600 per ticket). In comparison, the airfare for Grandma to travel from Chicago to Portland would be around $300. So after discussing the options with Kathy, we came to the realization that it would work best to have Grandma Barbara come to our house to watch the boys.

Wednesday January 24th

Flight to Tampa

On our departure day, we said goodbye to our boys and Grandma Barbara – realizing that we would return home with the answer to the million dollar question. As Kathy and I traveled to the airport, our discussion was casual, yet optimistic, with a couple joking references to coming home a millionaire. We wish we could have invited the whole family, but we realized that we would be very busy with all the media events.

Certainly, we would miss the boys – especially when it came time to share in the celebration of making the kick. And even if I missed the kick, the carefree attitude of a child might be the right prescription to put things in perspective. Nonetheless, we would be traveling to Tampa that day without our boys.

Welcome to Tampa

When we arrived at the airport, we were greeted by representatives from the Hershey Public Relations staff (Mike Kinney and Sue Karli). I had previously spoken with Mike about our arrival at the airport – he would be the guy holding a sign that said "Dan Kaler, Hershey Million Dollar Kick." As promised, we spotted Mike at the gate and we exchanged casual conversation about our trip. As we walked out of the terminal, Mike mentioned that a couple local television stations would video our arrival and perform a brief interview near the baggage claim area. And from there, we would tour Tampa in the Hershey Kissmobile (an extended-length vehicle in the shape of three giant Hershey Kisses).

While conducting the interview, I again stated my desire to share the cash prize with others. It just seemed right to make this statement – I really hoped that my message of generosity would have an impact on the viewers of the local television stations.

Dinner at Landry's Steakhouse

After the Kissmobile dropped us off at our hotel, we joined other Hershey staff at Landry's Steakhouse. While we were there, I spotted Antonio Freeman (wide receiver for the Green Bay Packers). I mentioned my celebrity spotting to Mike Kinney and he voluntarily stopped by Antonio's table. Apparently, Mike gave Antonio a brief summary of the Hershey contest and mentioned that I was a diehard

Packer fan. Moments later Antonio stopped by our table to say hello and offered me good luck wishes. It was just another special gesture to add to my million dollar memories.

Thursday January 25th

Meet the Press

The Hershey's public relations staff arranged several radio interviews for Thursday. All of the national radio broadcasters were gathered at the Tampa Hotel & Convention Center and they set up their interview equipment along several rows of tables that were aptly named "Media Row"

Mike and Mike

My first interview was scheduled with the "Mike & Mike Show" on ESPN radio (featuring Mike Golic and Mike Greenberg). John Carney would also participate in the interview to discuss his role in the contest. But since this interview would precede John Carney's kicks, we were uncertain of the actual distance of the Hershey Million Dollar Kick.

During the interview, John explained that he would attempt kicks from 50, 55 and 60 yards later that morning. For each successful kick, I would be able to move 5 yards closer for the Hershey Million Dollar Kick. Since the starting distance for my kick would be 40 yards, it was possible that the Hershey Million Dollar Kick could be as close as 25 yards if John made all three attempts, or as far as 40 yards if he missed all three attempts. John stated that he was ready for the challenge and that his kicks today would not be as stressful as an NFL game.

The interview was conducted in a very friendly and relaxed manner. I noticed a sense of brotherhood between Mike Golic and John Carney because they both played football at the University of Notre Dame. The interview started out with serious discussion about the contest, and then it got more light-hearted from there.

For instance, both Golic and Greenberg jabbed John about the importance of making his kicks so that I would have a better chance at the million dollars. In particular, they acted like a team of defense attorneys when they cross-examined John about his comment that he would have less pressure than a real NFL game.

Also, it was quite apparent that Mike Golic enjoyed the assort-ment of complimentary candy provided by the Hershey staff. It got quite comical with Greenberg roasting Golic about consuming all the Reese's Bites. It was good-natured humor, and if anything, it helped reduce the pressure of John's kicks that day.

Go, John, Go!

After the interview, we traveled with the Hershey staff to the outdoor arena (known as the NFL Experience) where John Carney would perform the official contest kicks. The NFL Experience was located adjacent to the site of the Super Bowl (Raymond James Stadium) and served as a festival of fun for football fans. There were several activities designed for fans to simulate the necessary talents of a professional football player, as well as an entertainment stage for live musical performances.

As we walked to the Hershey Million Dollar Kick contest field at the NFL Experience, I noticed that John was warming up in the parking lot. Although the contest rules stated that John could not practice on the actual contest field, the parking lot or anywhere else was fair game. I was pleased to see that John was working hard to potentially make my kick a little closer. And from inside the contest area, John's practice kicks sounded as if there was a pistol range in the parking lot!

Along with John practicing his kicks, I also noticed several school buses driving into the parking lot. I was informed that the Hershey Public Relations staff had invited several local elementary schools to observe and cheer during John's kicks. Additionally, these children would get to meet and have lunch with Sheldon Quarles (a linebacker for the Tampa Bay Buccaneers). This was another fine example of the thoughtful nature of the Hershey Corporation. The children appeared to be very excited about their field trip and the opportunity to participate in the event.

After John completed his warm up, he walked over to the contest field to get a firsthand look at the field conditions. The field was 65 yards of plush green artificial turf with white yard lines striped like an official field. Additionally, the contest field had a single goal post with two referees standing nearby to verify if the kick passed through the uprights.

Next, I walked over with the Hershey staff to speak with John. John was very focused and seemed eager to help me out with his kicks. However, he did express some concern about the starting position for his 60 yard kick. In particular, he would have to start his approach to the ball from a mixture of grass and gravel. Because the contest field was only 65 yards long, there was not adequate turf for John's kick-off style approach (which would require a start position from about 70 yards away). This was just part of the field conditions and something that he would have to deal with – just like his clutch kicks in the 1985 muddy mess between the University of Notre Dame and the University of Southern California.

As part of the last minute details, we gathered with the representatives from the SFX event staff to confirm the progression of the qualifying kick attempts. The SFX staff would first announce John and myself, then announce the distance for each of John's kicks, and then provide a "kick by kick" summary. It had the feel of a real game and I was anxiously awaiting the outcome. We gave John our best wishes for success and then walked over to the sideline.

You 'Da Man, John!

To start out the competition, the SFX staff announced John Carney and they encouraged the school children to give John a loud cheer. John's first field goal attempt was from 50 yards. He looked very calm, and I could sense that he was in a state of deep concentration. When he kicked the football it sounded like the "booming noise" from a cannon as it sailed straight towards the goal post. The outcome of his kick was revealed as the field officials raised their hands upward to signal that the kick was good. So at this point, I would be able to move up to the 35 yard line for my kick. This distance would still be very difficult kick for me, but hey, it was closer than 40 yards

His next kick was from 55 yards. It was also well struck – it flew higher and farther than the first kick, but landed wide right of the goal posts. Even though the second attempt had failed, there was still one more opportunity to for John to help me out – the dreaded 60 yard kick.

If John were to make this next kick, then I would be at a much more comfortable distance of 30 yards. This would be a critical kick.

I could tell that John was concerned about the circumstances. Not only would he have to deal with a stiff wind, but also he would have to begin his approach to the football from a gravel area beyond the artificial turf.

To help establish his approach strides, John used a string line to more accurately measure the desired distance from the football tee to his starting point in the gravel surface. After locating this position, John made several walk through approaches to get a better feel for the traction and approach angle. From there, John patiently waited for the strong winds to slow down. Then at the right moment, John darted towards the football and sent the football in flight. The football was sailing straight towards the goal post. I was optimistic that it would carry the distance, but it landed right near the base of the goal post.

After John missed the 60 yard kick, I could tell that he was very disappointed and frustrated with his effort. He told me, "Sorry I didn't get the job done."

"That's okay," I replied. "It will make it a better challenge for me." I was reaching, but I needed to find some positive motivation to prepare for my kick.

Back to Media Row

After John performed his kicks, we spoke briefly about practice plans for Friday and then we traveled back to "media row" at the Tampa Convention Center. Once there, John and I would participate in separate activities – John would join other NFL kickers in a tribute to Lou Groza (a NFL Hall of Fame kicker) and I would join the Hershey Public Relations staff to perform additional interviews with the radio stations at media row.

Chris "Boomer" Berman

For me, one of the coolest sports announcers is Chris "Boomer" Berman – you may know him as the guy from ESPN who gives nicknames during their highlight shows. On Thursday afternoon, I spotted Chris Berman in the media row area. I walked over to him and we had a brief conversation that went something like this:

"Hello Mr. Berman, could I get a quick autograph?" I then extended a promotional folder that was prepared for the Hershey Million Dollar Kick.

"Sure," he replied. "Are you doing the Hershey kick this year?"

"That's right, I'm the lucky contestant," I answered.

Next, Mr. Berman asked, "So, where you from?"

I stated that I lived in southern Washington. He then mentioned that he and his wife recently traveled near this area to tour the Mount St. Helens Volcanic Museum. After some additional conversation, he officially dubbed me with a nickname. His formal proclamation went something like this, "Well, I'll refer to you as the 'Volcano Kicker' when your kick erupts through the goal posts." How cool – that definitely was one of the most memorable conversations during my million dollar journey!

Can I have your Autograph?

While waiting for the next interview to occur, I was able to spot several celebrities walking through media row. It was really cool to see some celebrities close up – Gale Sayers, Joe Montana and Garo

Yepremian. I wasn't able to get close enough to ask them, but it sure would have been exciting to say hello and ask for their autograph.

I can recall several times from my childhood when I received an autograph of a professional athlete (or even saw them play at the stadium). I remember that I was amazed to experience their greatness. And now as an adult, it was still thrilling to see a famous professional athlete.

Friday January 26th

The Fox & Friends Interview

I wasn't really keen on waking up early for another interview on Friday morning, but I knew it was part of the event promotion. So at 7:00 AM that morning, I met the Hershey Public Relations staff (Mike Kinney and Sue Karli) in the hotel lobby and then we traveled to a parking lot near Tampa Stadium to meet the producer of the Fox & Friends morning show. It was decided that I would do a brief interview with the morning host and then we would both try kicking the football between the equipment trailers in the parking lot. It was early, but it sounded like fun to me.

After providing a brief interview with the host of the Fox & Friends morning show (Brian Kilmeade), it was suggested that we perform our own competition for the television audience. As previously agreed, I went along with the plan and hoped that a live television appearance would be a good warm-up for the Hershey Million Dollar Kick.

The production crew for Fox & Friends morning show set up some traffic cones to serve as our field goal target. My first kick landed between the cones that were set up in parking lot, while Brian Kilmeade squirmed a grounder that took several bounces towards the cones. However, my next kick was severely hooked to the left and was headed towards several equipment trailers – incoming, look out! It was fun, but I was glad to have more time to prepare for the real million dollar kick.

CNN Interview

Later that day, I performed a live interview via satellite for a CNN daytime news program (CNN Today) which was hosted by Lou Walters and Natalie Allen. I was familiar with their show and was impressed with their cordial and entertaining delivery of the news. I was really excited to be their guest and was honored that my million dollar journey would be a topic for their show.

Since my interview would be conducted via satellite, the location of the interview could be conducted anywhere deemed suitable for satellite transmission (ideally an unobstructed and scenic area within Tampa). The CNN production staff decided that my interview would be conducted along a river bank overlooking downtown Tampa. The CNN production staff established the satellite feed from their equipment truck and they provided the necessary audio wires for my interview. Next, I performed an audio test to confirm the satellite transmission between our remote location and the CNN studio in Atlanta. I was now ready for my first global television appearance.

The interview opened with Lou Walters stating, "Well, if you don't have much interest in the Ravens or the Giants, perhaps you would like to just turn on the television to catch Dan Kaler before the game. He's going to try to win $1,000,000."

Next, Natalie Allen responded with the statement, "That's right. And he doesn't have to talk to Regis Philbin to do it. He doesn't have to answer any questions. But he has to kick a field goal." And then Natalie offered the following invitation to join their discussion, "Hi, Dan. Are you are nervous?"

I responded by stating, "You know, I was nervous initially. But each day, I am getting more used to the idea of being on national television and going for the million dollars."

Next, Lou inquired about my selection as a contestant and my advancement as the finalist for the Hershey Million Dollar Kick. And later, when questioned about my chances of making the Hershey Million Dollar Kick, I stated, "I'm more comfortable from a 25 to 30 yard range. On Sunday, I will be kicking from 35 yards, which will require more power and loft to carry it a further distance."

To conclude the interview, both Lou and Natalie offered their encouragement for a successful outcome. And I ended the interview with the following reply, "Well, thank you. It's very exciting. And I would like to thank Hershey's just for the opportunity to live out a dream."[7]

CHAPTER 6

Goodwill to All

Hospital Tour

Another activity planned during Super Bowl week involved a visit to the All Children's Hospital in St. Petersburg, Florida. At first, I wasn't sure why the Hershey Public Relations staff would include this activity as part of the Hershey Million Dollar Kick promotion. Then I was told about the philanthropic tradition of Milton Hershey, the founder of the Hershey Chocolate Company. I learned that Mr. Hershey endured a poor childhood prior to achieving millionaire status. And upon attaining this financial status, Mr. Hershey founded the Milton Hershey School for orphaned boys in 1909. It was this example of caring for children that established the tone for the company values.

So following the corporate standard, it was decided that both John Carney and myself would visit the hospital to spread cheer to children stricken with serious illness. Since John Carney was staying at another hotel, it was agreed that John would meet us at the hospital at 10:00 AM. From there, we would receive a tour of the hospital and then visit with several of the patients and their families.

After hearing about their health issues, I really was uncertain what to say to the children. What could I do to improve their quality of life? I felt somewhat embarrassed to mention my opportunity to kick for a million dollars to the children and their parents. I was really concerned about appearing as "better than thou" to a sick child confined to a hospital bed, or coming across as "richer than thou" for the parents dealing with expensive medical costs.

So after much consideration, I asked John about his thoughts on how to deal with this situation. I remember John telling me to just share the story of my million dollar opportunity and that the kids would be excited to talk with us. He also stated that our visit could help the children to temporarily put aside their own problems.

After meeting the first few children, I quickly discovered that they viewed John (a professional football player) and me (a million dollar contestant) as celebrity figures. I think that meeting someone who "made it to the big leagues" or even "made it to the contest" provided a spirit of optimism for their medical conditions. I was truly happy to spend time with the children and was certainly thankful to have John demonstrate how our visit could be uplifting to these children.

A Very Busy Day

The balance of the day would be very busy. The Hershey staff planned a practice session at Jesuit High School at 2:30 PM, and then we would travel back to the NFL Experience for another media event at 4:30 PM. From there, Kathy and I would travel back to the airport to pick up a rental car – we wanted our own vehicle to explore the area, and plus we needed to pick up Kathy's brother and his wife at the airport on Saturday. However, the first issue was finding food!

Danny Needs a New Pair of Shoes

On our way to locate a suitable fast food restaurant, John suggested that we stop by a sports store to look for new football cleats. I am somewhat embarrassed to mention this, but I was using baseball cleats for my kicking competition. Not that I knew any difference; I thought the main reason for wearing cleats was to obtain better traction. John recognized my misconception, and he knew that a minor change in my kicking equipment might make a difference in the outcome of my field goal attempt.

Although I had fairly good accuracy, the key issue was getting more distance on my kicks. At this point in my preparation, I very rarely made my attempts from 35 yards (probably a 5% success rate) and I was very concerned about finding a way to improve my chances. I was even considering purchasing steel toe work boots to help improve my kicking distance. My plan was to stay the course until Saturday, and then make an honest evaluation of my soccer style technique. If my distance did not improve, then I would change my strategy for brute force – a straight on kick with the assistance of steel toe work boots.

After making a pit stop at my favorite Scottish restaurant (McDonald's), we found a sports store that had a wide assortment of athletic shoes. John suggested that I select a shoe with a fairly low cleat height and a very snug fit. He mentioned that NFL kickers typically have a smaller size shoe on their kicking foot to obtain better feel and control of their kicks. I decided to select a pair of Nike soccer cleats that were one size smaller. Also, this shoe style had the laces located along the side of the shoe to provide a smoother kicking surface at the top of the foot. I brought the shoes to the front counter and opened my wallet, but John was adamant that this would be his gift to me. This was just another example of John's character.

Show me the Money!

Next, we stopped by a local football field (Jesuit High School) for another field goal practice session. I'm not sure if it was the new shoes, but I started to kick the football much stronger. I remember John telling me to kick the football as if I was kicking a soccer ball into a soccer goal. I think this helped me focus more on the middle section of the football. The key result was that I was able to drive the football farther by keeping my body lower and making solid contact with the football.

While we were practicing on the football field, the high school track coach was working with a couple sprinters and he occasionally watched my kick attempts. During a break in the action, he yelled over to us, "Is that the guy kicking for a million bucks?"

"Yeah, I'm the lucky guy," I replied.

Then he added, "If you make your kick, don't forget to tell the television reporter about your friends at Jesuit High School in Tampa, Florida."

I shouted back, "Yeah, I won't forget about you."

He responded, "Have you got an agent yet? Because a teacher can always use a side job!"

I jokingly replied, "Well, what's in it for me? Show me the money!"

He laughed and shouted back, "Well good luck and don't forget about Jesuit High School!"

Sharing the NFL Experience

After completing the practice session at the high school, we traveled back to the NFL Experience for another media event. For this event, both John and I would perform a short kicking exhibition and then the Hershey staff would invite the spectators to participate in a kicking contest. The kicking distance for this contest was set at 25 yards. And if the contestant was successful at this distance, then they would win a 5 pound Hershey chocolate bar.

It was fun to watch the contestants and see how they approached their opportunity. For the most part, the contestants opted for the traditional "straight-on" style. Some used a running start, while others simply walked toward the ball to attempt their kick. Only a select few used a soccer style technique, but these contestants were more successful at their field goal attempts.

It was very entertaining to watch their reactions to the outcome of their kick. You could sense that some people were willing to try their luck without any expectations, while other contestants were very serious about their attempt (and consequently, more disappointed after missing their kick). Along with watching their expressions, it was fun to hear the comments from their friends. Actually, it was hilarious to hear some of the responses. It varied from the funny comments ("Man, you kick like my Grandma") to frustrated outbursts ("We waited in line for 45 minutes to see that!").

For those contestants who made the 25 yard kick, the Hershey staff would announce their name, home city, and then present them with the 5 pound chocolate bar. One of the winners was a former college kicker from Ohio (probably around 50 years old) who used a "straight-on" style. He was thrilled to re-live his college days and you could sense that he was quite excited to participate in this competitive event. Another winner was a younger guy (mid - twenties) that used the soccer style approach. After he sent his kick through the uprights, he mentioned that he was a soccer player and that kicking the football was an easy task for him. It made me think – I wonder if I could use him as my designated kicker on Sunday?

CHAPTER 7

A Day of Rest

Saturday January 27th

After being on the go the past several days, I was ready for a change of pace. I still planned to practice kicking at the NFL Experience later in the afternoon, but my main goal was to get some mental relaxation – the chance to sleep longer that morning, explore the local shopping mall, and dine at a nice restaurant. The only other task was to stop by the airport to pick up Kathy's brother (Mark Zipoy) and his wife (Tammy Zipoy) at the airport.

A Friend in my Corner

I was glad to have Kathy's brother (Mark Zipoy) with me. He displayed the classic definition of the "can do" attitude in just about everything. Mark was a very skilled carpenter who performed just about every task with a high intensity effort. Whether it was framing a house, offering hospitality to others, or even playing Monopoly – he consistently showed an energetic, winning attitude. And just like a prize fighter having a veteran trainer in his corner, I was glad to have him with me.

A Leisurely Lunch

After picking up Mark and Tammy at the airport, we stopped at a local restaurant for lunch and we discussed the events leading up to the Hershey Million Dollar Kick. As we summarized my million dollar journey, I found myself thinking that the past few weeks were too crazy to believe. I had been so busy that I really did not have the time to consider the whole story of my journey. And upon putting all the events in one conversation, I really felt overwhelmed with excitement and anticipation. I finally had to make a request that we keep our conversation low key. Thankfully, we changed our conversation to the latest news about our children and other family issues.

A Leisurely Practice

We arrived at the NFL Experience later that afternoon. Since I did not have any required appearances or interviews, we were able to take some time to observe the exhibits and activities at the NFL Experience. And later, we walked over to the location of the practice kick area to have a light workout session with John Carney. I felt really loose during the practice session and was kicking the football very well. Both John and I were satisfied with my progress to that point.

As we were leaving the NFL Experience that evening, we walked over to the field that would be used for the Hershey Million Dollar Kick. We noticed that the goal post had been moved to the opposite end of the field. Earlier in the week, John Carney had kicked with the wind (from north to south); however, the field goal post was now positioned in the north end zone. Since the wind direction was supposed to change that night, it appeared that this change might work to my advantage. Certainly the warm southerly winds would be welcome, but I was hoping for a wind reminiscent of my collegiate days in Wyoming.

As I walked onto the field, I had the sense that 35 yards on this field was a lot longer than the practice area. This was probably because the practice area was much narrower and gave the appearance of a tunnel leading to the goal post. I knew that the distance was the same on each field, but a wider field made the goal post look like an even bigger giant to conquer!

The Higher Goal

As I walked underneath the goal post, I had the sense that the cross bar appeared higher than usual. I recall saying to my wife, "I think the cross bar is too high!"

"Why, how high should it be?" she questioned.

"I think the top of the cross bar should be 10 feet," I replied.

To double check the height, I decided to take a running jump and see if I could touch the cross bar. From my basketball experiences, I knew that I could grab the rim on a 10 foot basketball hoop. In fact, I could dunk a tennis ball on most rims and sometimes even a deflated volley ball. So I took a running start and leaped for the goal post – to my surprise I was not able to slap the post. I decided to try one more time. This time I took a longer running start, and still, I was not able to touch the goal post. Thus, I concluded that the cross bar of the goal post was indeed higher than 10 feet.

Upon pointing this out to the Hershey staff, they mentioned that they would have someone measure the exact height. I showed my discovery to John Carney and asked for his clarification on the dimensions of the goal post. He concurred that the top of the cross bar should be 10 feet above the ground.

Upon closer examination, it appeared that the base of the field goal post was seated higher in the ground because the concrete footing was too shallow. Whatever the cause, I decided to not let this issue get the best of me. I was feeling confident about my kick and another 6 inches in height was not going to stop me!

CHAPTER 8

The Million Dollar Day

Before breakfast that morning, I spent some time reading the Bible and then went to the outdoor pool for a cool morning swim. It was rather cool that time of day and I was the only person in the pool. I was okay with the cold water and the isolated setting – this would help invigorate my physical and mental state.

While swimming I focused on developing an awareness of the importance of this day. This was my one time shot and I wanted to develop maximum focus on my kick. I imagine that other professionals commonly seek to attain this type of mental focus – a salesman preparing a presentation for a major client, a politician preparing his speech for a political debate, or an NFL coach reviewing his game plan for the Super Bowl. After this brisk swim, I went back to the room to shower and get dressed for the event.

For my national television appearance, I contemplated wearing a shirt from our church youth group – the front had the logo of our church and the back had the words "ALL THE TIME" in bold capital letters. When I was serving as a Sunday school teacher for the junior high students, we had the ritual that when a person would say, "God is good" then the other person would respond with the phrase "All the time." Alternatively, when someone started with the phrase "All the time" then the other person would complete this statement with "God is good." It was a great way to pump up the kids and have them focus on the reality of a living God.

Although I seriously considered wearing this shirt, I decided to follow the corporate line and wear the Hershey jersey that was provided at the preliminary competition in San Diego. However, there was another article of clothing that I had to wear – my old grey sweat shorts. These originally were full length sweat pants that I purchased in 1987 (the year I met my wife) and eventually I had to cut them off at the knees since they were ripped from years of use.

Over the years, these shorts had endured many of my athletic events and they had become part of my official athletic dress code.

The Super Bowl Warm-up

After having brunch at a local hotel, we stopped by the hotel gift shop to pick up some Super Bowl souvenirs. Not only did we pick up a few items for ourselves, but we also wanted to bring home some gifts for several people back home – the manager of the indoor soccer center, Greg Stoller, our church pastor, and Rian Lindell. Even if I did not come home a millionaire, I wanted to offer some type of gift to those people who contributed to my million dollar journey.

We departed the hotel at 10:30 AM and arrived at the NFL Experience at 11:15 AM (approximately 2.5 hours prior to the scheduled time for the Hershey Million Dollar Kick). The plan was to arrive early and devote at least 90 minutes for a practice session at the Hershey kicking area.

It was a warm, sunny morning and I felt the excitement in the air! I felt good – I had food in my belly, positive thoughts in my mind, and the chance to become a millionaire in just a few hours. I had my wife with me to provide emotional encouragement and John

Carney was there to provide final technical instruction.

Final Practice

I spent a good 15 minutes stretching out and felt ready for the

big day. Similar to my prior practice sessions, I began kicking from

20 yards and gradually worked my way back to the 35 yard distance.

I was very cautious to take my time and focus on striking the ball

well on every kick. As I recall, I attempted about 8 kicks from the

20, 25 and 30 yard distances. I was successful on about 75% of my

kicks thus far, and I was ready for the 35 yard distance.

As I walked over to place the ball in the kicking tee, I noticed

that the crowd was growing larger and cheering louder with each

successful kick. Although it was reassuring to have the support of

the crowd, I realized that I would need to block out their cheers and

focus on my technique.

For me, the key issues involved making a smooth approach to

the football, landing my plant foot in the right location, and striking

the football correctly. It was also helpful to visualize the football as a soccer ball and anticipate the familiar thump sound. After placing the football in the tee, I stood up and faced the goal post. I knew that 35 yards would be quite a stretch for me – I felt like I was facing my own Goliath (the giant goal post).

I felt that I pursued all the necessary steps. Along with putting forth the physical effort in my daily practices, I sought the counsel of others to prepare both my mind and body. Additionally, I prayed and asked others to pray for the gift of athletic ability. I was ready for the next challenge.

It was now time for a test – I paced back to line up my first practice kick from 35 yards. Slowly I rocked back and forth for a brief moment to collect my thoughts, and then started my approach to the football. First, I made a short jab step, then lunged forward with my next step to gain momentum, then landed my plant foot smoothly and struck the ball on the sweet spot. After making contact, I heard the familiar thump and watched the ball travel end over end towards the goal post. The ball appeared to be on course and I waited intently to see if it would carry far enough – it might be, it could be, it's good! I recall pumping my fist and hearing the crowd cheer with excitement at my accomplishment. At that moment, I realized that I could do it!

From there, I made 4 out of the next 8 kicks from 35 yards. I was having a blast – looking back now, I think this was one of my favorite moments of the event. To help me prepare even more, I decided to back up 3 more yards to make it a longer kick. John noticed my intentions and cautioned me not to over work myself, but I felt ready for another challenge.

As I moved back, I was standing closer to the crowd and I could sense their interest in my kicks. At this point, I felt like I was on center stage – my pride was on the line and my desire to succeed was pushed to a higher level. With each subsequent attempt, I took my time and viewed each kick as the Hershey Million Dollar Kick. Out of the next six kicks from 38 yards, I was successful on two attempts (with a couple near misses). At this point, I wanted to finish with a successful kick. With my next kick, I focused intently on my technique and successfully sent the football through the goal posts. I looked over to John and confidently stated, "I think I'm ready."

John replied back saying. "You are doing great! I think you're ready too."

Encouraging Words

And with each successful kick during my warm up, I could sense that my wife was getting excited about my chances of making the kick. Not only did I feel good about my improved kicking ability, but I was pleased that my wife recognized the fruit of my efforts. To this day, one of the most satisfying remarks that I received from Kathy was her comment, "I'm so proud of you, Dan!" For me, her words of love and encouragement would far outweigh my thoughts of being a millionaire.

I could also notice a sense of optimism from the Hershey staff. There were definitely times when we all had doubts about making a kick from 35 yards. My first day at the NFL Experience did not look that promising, but my kicking abilities had definitely improved since that first day. And now, I could see Mike smiling a little more and Sue seemed more optimistic about the outcome. After a successful field goal, Sue would say, "Awesome, Dan!"

And Mike would cautiously remark, "Save that one for the real kick."

Then I jokingly jabbed back with the phrase, "Show me the money!"

Thankfully, all the Hershey staff were on my side. Since the Hershey Company had secured an insurance policy for the million dollar payout, they were all hoping for a successful kick. They had already made their financial investment in this promotion, and a successful kick would provide more media exposure for the company. In fact, they mentioned that a successful kick would bring multiple interview opportunities; Good Morning America, Jay Leno and maybe David Lettermen. So along with a million dollar prize, I was really looking forward to perhaps meeting David Letterman and kicking footballs with him in the alley behind the Late Night Theatre.

Finding Peace

After I concluded my warm up, I asked John and his wife to pray with me. We found a somewhat quiet area of the NFL Experience to take a few moments to ask for God's blessing on my kick. I cannot exactly recall the content of their prayers, but I felt honored to have John and his wife pray for me that day. As for my prayer, I again asked God for athletic ability, emotional strength, and regardless of the outcome, that I would be pleasing to Him.

It was now about 1:00 PM – only 45 minutes to the kick. I rested for about 15 minutes and then decided to keep active to relieve any jitters. I recall a similar situation on our wedding day when I was playing football with my groomsmen until an hour before the wedding ceremony. So to help keep relaxed during this million dollar day, I decided to kick a soccer ball with my brother-in-law, and later I kicked a football into a stationary net.

At around 1:35 PM, (just 10 more minutes before my appearance on national television), the Hershey staff stated that it was time to walk over to the contest field. At John's suggestion, I decided to use ear plugs to minimize the crowd noise. And as we started the short walk to the contest field, I began humming a simple tune to help myself relax and maintain focus. It was just a slow chorus of repeating the word "Hal-le-lu-iah, Hal-le-lu-iah, Hal-le-lu-iah" over and over

again. At that moment, I felt at peace and ready for the kick.

Pre-Kick Interview

Before I would perform my kick, there would be one other

distraction. As part of the CBS Pre-game Show, I would perform

a live interview with the CBS field announcer, Craig James. Much

to my dislike, this interview would occur just prior to the national

telecast of the Hershey Million Dollar Kick

I really did not like the idea of the pre-kick interview – I would

rather perform my kick and then speak with the announcer. But the

Hershey staff indicated that it would be a brief interview and that

most of the questions would be directed to either John or Kathy.

Although I was glad to have John handle the bulk of the questions, I

really wanted to just kick the football as soon as possible.

With only a couple minutes until the live telecast, I walked to

the spot of the 35 yard kick. My initial thought was that the 35 yard

distance seemed longer than my 35 yard kicks in the practice area.

I decided to back up to the 40 yard distance to fix my eyes on that distance, and then move up to the 35 yard line. This technique helped give me a better outlook for the 35 yard distance, but I still needed a powerful kick.

One Minute Warning

When I returned to the sideline, I heard the CBS Director call out, "One minute to live." I stood in the assigned position next to Craig, John and Kathy. Although Craig was in constant conversation with the CBS Production staff, I was able to have a final conversation with Kathy and John.

Kathy leaned over to give me a hug, "Good luck, honey!"

"I'll give it my best," I replied.

Then John offered final encouragement, "I think you're gonna do it!"

Suddenly over the public address speakers, the CBS Director shouted, "Fifteen seconds to live."

Upon hearing this announcement, my adrenaline started to flow. I got a quick dose of stage fright – as if my elementary school teacher just called me in front of the classroom to solve a problem on the chalkboard. As I looked over at Craig, I heard the CBS Director

rattle off the countdown, "And 5, 4, 3, 2, 1 ... we're live!"

Craig: We're live at the NFL Experience for the Hershey Million Dollar Kick. And a guy that is about to become a millionaire is standing next to me. This is going to be a great day for you. Dan Kaler, are you excited about this?

Dan: Yeah, it's like a dream come true.

Craig: Well, you got some support staff over here – John Carney of the San Diego Chargers and your wife Kathy. There have been two winners in the last five years, do you think you can do it?

Dan: Let's keep the streak going.

Craig: Go for it out there! Good luck to you.

Craig: On Thursday, John Carney kicked field goals from 50, 55 and 60 yards. And for each successful attempt, Dan could move 5 yards closer. Carney made one, so this kick will be from 35 yards away.

Craig: John, what's the one thing that you told Dan to really keep in mind here?

John: Dan's a great athlete, I told him just to drive through the ball and be proud of your kick.

Craig: Now how wide is that goal post? It looks pretty wide out there.

John: It's a little over 18 feet.

Craig: Kathy, I'm a little nervous.

Kathy: I am too![8]

So off I went to the middle of the field with the football in hand, jogging with the gait of a warrior ready for battle, and hoping for the kick of a lifetime. As I got closer to the kicking tee, I started a quick series of "high knee pumps" to get loose and release some of the nervous energy. Next, I bent down to place the football in the kicking tee and paced back three strides to align my kick towards the goal posts. I then returned to the tee to improve the lateral tilt of the football.

As I stood over the football, I could hear the crowd shouting, "Let's go, Dan! Let's go, Dan! Let's go, Dan! " At first I really appreciated the encouragement, but then it got to a point when I realized that I did not deserve their praise. So to redirect the focus to my source of strength, I pointed my hand up to the sky and softly said to myself, "It's not for me, give it up for God." And with that proclamation, I was ready to get on with my kick.

My set-up routine was the same as my warm up session earlier that day. I stood behind the football, backed up three paces, pointed towards the football with both hands, and then extended my arms towards the goal posts to establish the proper alignment. Next, I took a deep breath, moved two side-steps to my left, and stood in that resting spot while rocking my hands in an underhand motion. I knew that I had to develop optimal forward momentum and I was waiting for the right time to begin my approach to the football (similar to waiting for the ideal time to hop into a swinging jump rope).

I could no longer hear the crowd. My heart was beating rapidly. Now was my chance to kick for a million dollars. I started my approach to the football – first a small jab step, next a strong stride with my right leg, followed by a final stride with my left foot landing next to the football. Then I swung my right foot downward, swept the football off the kicking tee, and sent the football towards the goal post.

I often thought about how I would react after seeing the results of my kick. If I was successful, then I was ready to allow the over-whelming sense of joy to take over – sprinting towards the goal posts, leaping wildly, pumping my fists, and then running towards the crowd to exchange high fives as I circled the perimeter of the entire field! Perhaps that is how it will feel to enter the gates of Heaven! And if I missed the kick, then I just wanted to act with honor – to be thankful for the opportunity, to not show any anger, and to be proud of my effort.

After following through with my kicking foot, I caught the ball in mid-flight and noticed that it was rapidly spinning end over end – an indicator that I hit the ball too low. Then I observed that the path of the football was headed wide right of the goal post. At that point, I knew that I had missed the kick.

The Post Game

I continued to watch the flight of the football as it sailed wide right about 5 yards from the upright and hit the Hershey Kissmobile which was parked next to the goal post. Realizing that my journey had ended that day, I slapped my hands together, shook my head in disappointment, and then walked over to Craig James for the post-kick interview.

Craig: Hey, nice try Dan. You know, you really don't lose in this thing.

Dan: Yeah, it's been a joy to be here.

Craig: Were you nervous?

Dan: Not too bad.

Craig: Well, when you go back and look at the replay, it looks like you got under the kick a little bit.

Dan: Yeah, just a little too forward on the toe.

Craig: Were you more nervous than you thought you would be?

Dan: Actually, through the power of prayer, I've been pretty at ease.

Craig: You really don't lose in this thing. Let's bring in the Hershey's Vice President of Marketing, Al Germann, to present the check.

Al Germann: Thanks Craig. Dan, you and John have been working so hard on this thing. Millions of fans were rooting for you. All of the Hershey Foods employees were rooting for you. But we still have a check for you for $10,000. Congratulations.

Dan: Thank you Hershey! It's been a wonderful dream come true. Thanks for the opportunity!

Craig: Let's bring in Kathy. You have two boys waiting back home, and going home with $10,000 is a good experience.

Kathy: Absolutely, it's been a great time. We've enjoyed it![9]

The Mulligan

After the post-kick interview, I decided to take another try at 35 yards. I knew that I missed out on the cash, but now it was for pride. It was an instinctive decision – I never asked if I could take an extra kick, but I wanted another chance to split the uprights. It was similar to taking another shot in golf when you are not satisfied with the outcome of your first shot (commonly know as "taking a mulligan").

I turned towards Kathy and John to declare my decision, "I'm gonna take another try."

Kathy looked shocked and said, "What are you doing?"

"I'm gonna try again. I want to see if I can make it," I replied. I was not ready to walk off the field yet.

John responded with a smile and a head nod – I think he understood my motive for a second chance.

I returned to field with the same ammunition (the football), although this time I had a renewed ambition (competitive pride) for a successful kick from 35 yards. There were still spectators watching from the bleachers and the Hershey executives remained gathered near the sideline. Although I was no longer on national television, I felt more determined to make the kick.

I did not spend as much time thinking about this next kick. I quickly went through my pre-kick routine and paced over to my starting point. I charged the football with even greater momentum, but this time my foot came across the football to set the direction of flight to the left of the goal post. As I watched the football travel off course, I knew that this was not my best effort. I must try one more time.

My brother-in-law retrieved the football and threw it back to me. I took a deep breath to slow down and get ready for one last kick. I decided to tone down my intensity and just make a smooth approach to the football. Although I did not develop the same level of forward momentum, I made fairly good contact with the football. The football sailed straight towards the goal post, and was rapidly traveling end over end. The only question was whether it would have enough distance to clear the cross bar.

I was gaining optimism as the ball approached the goal post. I could hear cheers of anticipation from those people still gathered around the field. As I watched the football making the final descent, the next sound I heard was the dreaded "bonk" tune of the football striking a metal surface. In this case, the football struck the middle of the cross bar and bounced back towards me. In unison, the crowd voiced an "oooh" groan. Both Kathy and John looked over to express their amazement of this near miss. All I could do was shake my head and smile.

After this final "mulligan" kick attempt, I performed an interview for the private video production agency employed by the Hershey Company. This video crew had been filming most of my practice sessions during the week and they observed my improved progress during the week. I had spoken with their interviewer several times during the week, and I felt very comfortable expressing my feelings with him. When asked how I felt about my near miss on the "mulligan" kick, I stated that hitting the cross bar confirmed that today was not my day to become a millionaire.

My initial measurement for a successful outcome was based on the number of zeros following the number "1" on my contest paycheck (with 1,000,000 as the only option for success). However, my "mulligan" attempt revealed that the purpose of my journey was not intended to provide a million dollar payout – there would be a greater purpose.

CHAPTER 9

The Aftermath

After wrapping up the post-kick interview, I had a final conversation with the Hershey executives to express my gratitude for the Hershey Million Dollar Kick experience. Additionally, I thanked John Carney for his coaching efforts and his friendship – I really enjoyed getting to know the man behind the football player. Next, I grabbed the football and asked my brother-in-law to play catch for a while. It was a much needed opportunity to take a deep breath, get away from the spotlight, and get back to the simple task of having fun throwing the football.

After Mark and I concluded our game of "quarterback challenge," we decided to move onto the more important joy of finding our wives among the remaining spectators. Next, we departed the NFL Experience for a rather long walk to a pre-game tailgate party. During our walk, I called my Dad on a cell phone to discuss the results of my kick. I was still coming to terms with the disappointment of missing the kick and I thought a talk with Dad would be helpful. I don't recall the whole conversation, but I distinctly remember my Dad emphasizing that he was thrilled to watch my appearance on national television and he was very proud of how I conducted myself that day. His loving words served as a "cell phone hug" to relieve some of my sorrow.

Would have, Could have, Should have ...

As we continued our walk to the tailgate party, my thoughts soon reverted back to my failed kick. When reviewing the final moments before my kick, I remember thinking to myself, "I've gotta develop a lot of power. I'm gonna strike the football with incredible force." And now recalling these two sentences, I realize that I was pressing too much. This was similar to my experiences as a golfer when trying to blast a drive from the first tee – trying to out muscle a golf ball, and then hooking it into the rough. If only I would have slowed down a bit, played it cool and showed more confidence in my ability.

The more I thought about the outcome, I questioned why God did not "step in" to grant a successful kick. If God could help Moses separate the Red Sea, then surely he could have provided a gust of wind to send the football on the right course. However, for reasons unknown to me, my desire for a successful kick was not fulfilled that day.

Upon arriving at the tailgate party, my thoughts were temporarily directed towards the vast assortment of food – several choices of barbeque, salads, fruit and plenty of deserts. We selected our entrée items and joined some of the Hershey staff. At first, the topic of our discussion focused on other issues; our favorite food items, which team would win the Super Bowl, or identifying celebrities in the crowd. However, several other people at the tailgate party would occasionally approach me to ask if I was the "Million Dollar Contestant" (my Hershey football jersey must have sparked their interest). In a humble manner, I would confirm their inquiry and then inform them that I missed the kick that day. After several inquiries, I soon discovered that my identity as "the guy who missed the kick" was not very uplifting for me – at this point, I was ready to leave the tailgate party and get to the Super Bowl game.

Game Time

As part of the contest prize package, I received two tickets for the Super Bowl game. Initially, the plan was that Kathy and I would attend the game. I was hopeful that attending the game together would be a good way to celebrate a memorable day. But with the outcome of the kick that day, we decided that Mark and I would attend the game. In the meantime, our wives would return to the hotel for a casual evening of dining and shopping.

As Mark and I approached the stadium, we noticed several people trying to buy tickets. Some of the offers were as high as $3,000 for a ticket! I had to stop and think about it – would it be respectable sell the tickets that Hershey provided as a gift? After some thought, I realized that attending the game and honoring their gift was the right decision.

Upon entering the stadium, we could feel the excitement in the air. Before the start of the game we were treated to a classic song by Ray Charles singing with his unique style, "America, America, God done shed his grace on thee." And then, as the Backstreet Boys sang the National Anthem, we were amazed to see a Stealth fighter jet fly over the stadium. Lastly, the pre-game festivities concluded as the players were introduced to the flash of fireworks bursting overhead. It was now game time!

Unfortunately, the football game did not follow the same level of pre-game excitement. The Baltimore Ravens defense limited the New York Giants offense quite handily that day. The only scoring play for the Giants was a kick-off return for a touchdown in the second half, but that was quickly equaled by a similar kick-off return by the Ravens. The Baltimore Ravens went on to beat the Giants by a score of 34 -7. The worst thing was that the uneventful pace of the game provided more idle time for me to think about missing my kick.

True Friends

During the drive home from the game, I called both my brother (Mark Kaler) and sister (Lori Kaler) who were both hosting Super Bowl parties at their homes. My brother was living in the Chicago area and my sister was living near Alexandria, Virginia. I knew they were excited about their "little brother" having a chance to win a million dollars, but I hoped that missing my kick did not let them down.

I decided to wait until after the game in order to have a more subdued conversation with them. When speaking with my brother, he was very supportive and emphasized the importance of enjoying the moment regardless of the outcome. Next, I called Lori – I knew that she would be more emotional with her reaction. She mentioned that all her friends at the party were excited for me and were impressed with my appearance on national television. She mentioned that she really thought that I would make the kick and she was concerned about how I was feeling about missing the kick. I reassured her that I was doing fine and to not worry about me. It was helpful to speak with my brother and sister – I felt that I had a better handle on the outcome of my kick.

Upon returning to the hotel, Mark Zipoy and I compared notes with our wives regarding the game that evening. Kathy and Tammy mentioned that they watched part of the game at a restaurant, but quickly became bored by the dominance of the Ravens. Mark and I both agreed that the game could have been better – like if the Green Bay Packers had played in the Super Bowl!

While we were hanging out in the room, the Hershey Public Relations staff called and asked if they could stop by our room for a late night pizza. Some food and friendly conversation sounded good to us, so we had our own private post-game party with Mike Kinney, Sue Karli, and Mark McCormick (Marketing Manager). While we were enjoying the pizza, we also shared several memories from the past few days – all the media interviews, the celebrities that we met along the way, and even my "mulligan" kick that hit the cross bar.

Along with bringing the pizza, the Hershey staff also provided some officially sanctioned Super Bowl XXXV souvenirs. I was very surprised to receive these additional gifts, but the most significant gift was a miniature football. Upon receiving this gift, I asked that they all sign the football as a reminder of their friendship during my million dollar experience. Although I had collected several autographs from sports celebrities that week, it was the signatures from my Hershey friends that I valued the most.

Back to Reality

After tossing and turning most of the night, I woke up the following morning with the realization that my million dollar opportunity was in the past. I still felt the sting of disappointment, but I was ready to travel back home and get back to normal life. Now was the time to cast my disappointment aside and live out one of my favorite Bible verses, "Rejoice and be glad, for this is the day the Lord has made!" (Psalm 118:24). It was quite apparent to me that I had to drop my disappointment of yesterday and focus on the simple gifts of each day.

One helpful step was a phone conversation with a radio talk show in Chicago. When I had previously lived in the Chicago area, I enjoyed listening to the Spike O'Dell Radio Show on WGN radio.

Spike would commonly provide a clean cut, carefree, and humorous insight on the simple things of life. After we moved to Washington state, I was not able to listen to the radio show, but I would periodically ask my brother-in-law about the latest happenings on the Spike O'Dell Radio Show.

As a surprise to me that morning, Mark decided to call Spike's radio show from our hotel room. As I later found out, Mark had called the radio show prior to traveling to Tampa and he arranged the phone interview for that morning. We both spoke with Spike via a conference call format to summarize the events from Super Bowl Sunday. Our interview with Spike was helpful in recapping the positive events – attending a national sports event, participating in the Hershey Million Dollar Kick, and developing new friendships. I also gained a better appreciation for Mark's friendship and his willingness to travel to Florida to accompany me for the kick.

Flight back home

It was now time to leave for the airport. Upon arriving at the departure gate, we joined the multitude of Super Bowl fans making their journey back home. Along with our carry-on baggage, I now had an oversized check for $10,000 that I had to stow onboard the airplane. So much for traveling anonymously!

While we were waiting for the outbound flight, we had a rather lengthy conversation with the sister of one of the Baltimore Raven players. She stated that her brother was a reserve offensive lineman and she also commented that several Raven players were devout Christians.

Eventually, we discussed my participation in the Hershey Million Dollar Kick. Upon hearing about our disappointment of missing the kick, she had an interesting response – she commented that the outcome must have been God's plan. Her view was that if it was meant to happen, then surely God would have made it happen. I found these remarks enlightening – perhaps I should stop my nagging thoughts about missing the kick, and realize there was a greater purpose.

When we boarded the plane, I was seated next to a father and son that were wearing the official Super Bowl XXXV shirts. During the flight, they had several conversations about their Super Bowl trip. I joined the conversation to discuss a variety of issues – where were your seats at the game? Which team did you want to win? Was that a boring game or what?

And later, I shared the outcome of my million dollar kick opportunity. They both seemed excited to hear the story and they asked several questions about the contest. When I mentioned my disappointment about missing the kick, the father had the following response, "Even though you missed the kick, it sounds like a great experience for you. And plus you came home with $10,000." His reply brought back the idea of being content and to not overlook the blessings that I had received during the past few weeks.

My Church Family

Prior to leaving for the Super Bowl, our pastor (Dave McCabe) had asked if he could meet us at the airport when we returned from the Super Bowl. Whether I made the kick or not, I thought it would be helpful to be with our pastor when we arrived at the airport. His spiritual support would provide a "safe landing" for our return back home.

While we had a layover in Dallas during our return flight, I called Pastor Dave to confirm our arrival time. I mentioned that our connecting flight was delayed and that we would arrive later that night. He asked if he could give us a ride home from the airport and I graciously accepted his offer. Pastor Dave also asked if a few people from church could also meet us at the airport – I also welcomed this offer and was thankful for our church family.

Upon arriving at the airport, we were warmly greeted by Pastor Dave and his wife at the arrival gate. We exchanged hugs and had a brief conversation with other friends from church. As we walked to the baggage claim area, I realized that our Pastor and our church friends were offering their unconditional love – the outcome of my kick did not matter to them, and they still showed their love to us. Wow, that's cool to think about even now! As a Christian, I think that this type of brotherly love provides a window to better under-stand God's love for us.

While driving from the airport, Pastor Dave and his wife mentioned that a local television film crew (KOIN-TV, the CBS affiliate) attended the Sunday morning church service. Previously, I had conducted an interview with the KOIN-TV sports anchor and I mentioned that my church was planning to watch the live broadcast of my kick which would occur just prior to the 11:00 AM service. Apparently, the KOIN-TV news producer had contacted Pastor Dave to verify if they could send a film crew to document our church congregation viewing and responding to my kick. And as it turned out, the KOIN-TV film crew attended the entire service and the final news segment conveyed a wonderful synopsis of the events at our church.

As we continued our drive home, Pastor Dave explained that the news segment opened with the church congregation singing praise songs before my kick. And even after my kick sailed wide right, the church congregation continued to sing praise songs. Rather than focus on the outcome of my kick, the KOIN-TV news segment correctly portrayed the "praise God in all situations" attitude during the church service. We all agreed that the television coverage provided a different slant than your average evening news program, and perhaps this news segment would have an impact on the viewers.

The Lawn Mower

As we approached our street, I was searching for a way to express to Pastor Dave that I was disappointed that I would not be able to contribute a larger portion towards our church construction project. I recalled a situation that he once shared about the limited church finances after the initial construction phase of our church. In response to the limited finances, Pastor Dave made a suggestion to have a special offering to fund the purchase of a new riding lawn mower. As it turned out, the church received offerings that would only cover a portion of the expense. However, the following week a stranger stopped by the church and made the statement, "I hear you need a lawn mower." Needless to say, our church graciously accepted his offer to buy a brand new riding lawn mower. And it was not your average lawn mower; the stranger was adamant that he buy the church a top of the line John Deere model.

After recalling this story, I realized the perfect way to express my thoughts. Staying with the lawn mower theme, I stated, "Well Pastor, sorry I didn't bring home a lawn mower." He looked over with a puzzled look at first, and then I reminded him about the stranger who bought the first riding lawn mower for the church. He nodded and smiled to let me know that he got the message. And to complete the story, the financing of our church expansion project would eventually occur a few years later through the generous contributions from our entire church congregation.

"All things work together for good to them who love God, to them who are called according to his purpose." (Romans 8:28)

CHAPTER 10

The Conclusion

It has now been six years since my million dollar kick landed wide right. Even though I have said farewell to my dreams of being an instant millionaire, I still wonder how it would feel to see my kick sail between the field goal posts.

Every Super Bowl weekend since 2001, I have returned to the local football field with my two sons to re-live the Hershey Million Dollar Kick. This is my chance to restore some old memories and kick a couple footballs through the uprights from 35 yards. Over the years, my sons have become familiar with the annual routine and the special rule for the day – "We can't leave the field until Dad makes one more kick." And now that they are older, my sons have joined me with their own kick attempts. Along with reminiscing about my million dollar experience, this annual event is a special day to recognize the many blessings of the past year and realize the continuation of God's plan for my life.

I have often reflected how my life would have changed if I had made the kick. Similar to the Christmas movie, "It's a Wonderful Life," – I would have my own guardian angel show me the consequences of the fork in the road. For instance, I may have become very materialistic after making my kick and my life may have taken a dramatic turn for the worse. And knowing that God's plan is better than my own desires, I am confident that being "wide right from 35 yards" has helped me become a better man. For at the end of my million dollar journey, I realized that God is more concerned about my spiritual growth than my financial growth.

No Pain, No Gain

Over the last six years, I have continued to play competitive sports as a means to quench my thirst for athletic joy. Although my efforts as a "weekend warrior" could never equal the thrill of kicking a million dollar field goal, I have enjoyed the sense of accomplishment, the brotherly bonding, and the physical exercise from my athletic activities. Unfortunately, I have incurred several injuries along the way (a broken thumb, a broken foot, and another broken foot). But there was an important benefit as a result of my injuries. These pitfalls provided some idle time for contemplating the big picture of life and compiling my thoughts for this book.

In 2005, I suffered a severe foot fracture known as a Lis-Franc dislocation fracture. The injury occurred while catching a touch-down pass in a flag football league – my joyous touchdown reception was quickly replaced with excruciating pain. The medical prognosis involved extensive surgery, followed by two weeks of bed rest and then six months of non-weight bearing activity. While recuperating at home, I was able to spend some time reviewing my life and the purpose of my million dollar kick experience. I considered writing my thoughts on paper, but I became distracted with other activities at home – namely, watching the NCAA basketball tournament and coaching little league baseball.

Then in 2006, I broke the same foot (this time a metatarsal frac-ture) while playing in the same flag football league. I again found myself with several weeks of idle time to recover from my latest injury – perhaps God was telling me that I should reconsider writing a book. And thus, my book writing adventure began at that time.

The Writing Begins

I began writing key statements to help provide perspective on the Hershey Million Dollar Kick experience. I started with the following two statements to develop an optimistic outlook after my unsuccessful kick:

- **I can find hope for the future and realize that God's plan for my life is better than obtaining any worldly treasure.**

- **I have a greater purpose than becoming a millionaire.**

And later, I compiled additional statements and identified Bible passages that provided a clearer understanding of a healthy relationship with God:

- **God is Good – the creator of all things and provider of all our needs.**

Shout for joy to the LORD, all the earth. Worship the LORD with gladness; come before him with joyful songs. Know that the LORD is God. It is he who made us, and we are his; we are his people, the sheep of his pasture. Enter his gates with thanksgiving and his courts with praise; give thanks to him and praise his name. For the LORD is good and his love endures forever; his faithfulness continues through all generations. (Psalm 100:1-5)

I am the good shepherd. The good shepherd lays down his life for the sheep. (John 10:11)

- **God works all things for our good.**

Delight yourself in the LORD and he will give you the desires of your heart. (Psalm 37:4)

If God is for us, who can be against us? (Romans 8:31)

- **God is deserving of our praise.**

Praise the LORD. How good it is to sing praises to our God, how pleasant and fitting to praise him! He heals the brokenhearted and binds up their wounds. He determines the number of the stars and calls them each by name. Great is our Lord and mighty in power; his understanding has no limit. (Psalm 147:1, 3-5)

My sheep listen to my voice; I know them, and they follow me. I give them eternal life, and they shall never perish; no one can snatch them out of my hand. My Father, who has given them to me, is greater than all; no one can snatch them out of my Father's hand. I and the Father are one. (John 10:27-30)

After writing these framework statements, I began documenting the events leading up to the Hershey Million Dollar Kick. The task of re-living my experience was quite enjoyable and therapeutic. And the compilation of this book manuscript brought greater clarity to my million dollar journey.

Ask Coach

Eventually, I came to a certain point in my writing where I wanted to seek counsel from someone who had persevered in a similar situation. And being a college football fan, I remembered that Florida State University was involved in three historic heart-break losses where the potential winning field goal kick landed wide right (commonly referred to as Wide Right I, Wide Right II, and Wide Right III). These experiences by Florida State University would be an ideal example of a team rebounding from a tough loss – and what better person to interview than Coach Bobby Bowden, Head Coach of Florida State University.

My first step was to check the Florida State University web site to obtain the mailing address for the athletic office. While browsing this web site, I was amazed to read about Coach Bowden's accomplishments – serving as Head Coach for over 30 years and the only coach in NCAA history to win 11 consecutive bowl games (1985-

95).[10] Upon learning more about Coach Bowden's illustrious career, I knew that he was a man who could provide great insight from his experiences.

After sending a letter describing my book writing quest, Coach Bowden graciously agreed to a telephone interview. During my interview with Coach Bowden, he offered three key statements that served to enlighten the development of my concluding thoughts:

> *Question: How do you view athletics?*
> COACH BOWDEN: It's a game, not a GOD. The game is a way to exhibit talent to glorify God.

> *Question: How would you describe the joy you receive from athletic victory?*
> COACH BOWDEN: Winning a football game is temporary happiness.
> Joy is different – it is a sustaining spiritual gift from God.

> *Question: How did you motivate your players after experiencing a tough loss?*
> COACH BOWDEN: It was a test of their coping skills. To get better, you must get up and move onward.

My Concluding Testimony

After reflecting on my million dollar experience and my interview with Coach Bowden, I identified additional scripture to drive home the essence of my book. In these concluding paragraphs, I leave you with the following testimony.

An Audience of One

I realize that some people regard athletics as a way to receive praise from others. As a child, I dreamed of playing professional sports in front of a packed stadium, making the game winning score, and hearing the applause of the fans. And later, I experienced the thrill of hearing the fans at Super Bowl XXXV cheer for the Hershey Million Dollar Kick. But the key step in my spiritual growth was realizing that I am living for God – an audience of one.

> *"Whatever you do, work at it with all your heart, as working for the Lord, not for men, since you know that you will receive an inheritance from the Lord as a reward. It is the Lord Christ you are serving." (Colossians 3:23-24)*

Pure Joy

Initially, I viewed the thrill of athletic accomplishment as joy. However, my discussion with Coach Bowden provided a key moment of clarity – that we can experience a sustaining joy greater than any athletic accomplishment.

The Hershey Million Dollar Kick experience was a thrilling journey that came to an abrupt end. But I have come to realize that my faith provides a sustaining joy greater than any worldly treasure.

> *Though you have not seen him, you love him; and even though you do not see him now, you believe in him and are filled with an inexpressible and glorious joy. (1 Peter 1:8)*

Moving Onward

After my kick attempt sailed wide right, I was very disappointed and was unsure of the purpose of my million dollar journey. Initially, my measure of success was different from God's plan for my life. But eventually, I realized that being "wide right" was a means of furthering my spiritual growth.

> *Consider it pure joy, my brothers, whenever you face trials of many kinds, because you know that the testing of your faith develops perseverance. Perseverance must finish its work so that you may be mature and complete, not lacking anything. (James 1: 2-4)*

Eternal Strength

I have come to realize that my journey in life will not merely involve navigation through level terrain, for there will be steep uphill climbs, as well as thrilling downhill adventures. But through the many turns in life, I have found that my time on earth is best spent praising God rather than dwelling on my frustrations or failures. And in conclusion, I have learned that even though I was wide right on my million dollar kick ... God is good!

"Those who hope in the Lord will renew their strength. They will soar on wings like eagles, they will run and not grow weary, they will walk and not be faint." (Isaiah 40 : 31)

Afterword by Bobby Bowden (The Extra Point)

Every living human being at one time in their life, or another, experiences a "Wide Right." If you have yet to experience one, brace yourself. How can God and/or man test your character without a "Wide Right?"

I learn more from losses than I do wins. Losses and wide rights make you self-analyze to find out where you are breaking down and get it corrected. I always go to God in prayer for help. God has never failed to answer my prayer and lead me along.

Look at Dan's life after his "Wide Right." Instead of receiving instant gratification that lasts only until the next game, he has found a joy that will last forever.

Lesson Learned? Make God your #1 priority in life, make your family #2 and then let football come where it may!

Coach Bobby Bowden

Florida State Football

References

[1] see http://www.profootballhof.com/hall/release.jsp?release_id=1859

[2] see http://www.packers.com/news/stories/2004/12/28/2/

[3] see http://baseball-almanac.com/box-scores/boxscore.php?boxid=198706200CHN

[4] Hershey Food Press Release, January 12, 2001

[5] Hershey Food Press Release, January 12, 2001

[6] The Columbian Newspaper, January 21, 2001

[7] see http://cnnstudentnews.cnn.com/TRANSCRIPTS/0101/26/tod.05.html

[8] CBS Super Bowl Pregame Show, January 28, 2001

[9] CBS Super Bowl Pregame Show, January 28, 2001

[10] see http://seminoles.cstv.com/sports/m-footbl/mtt/bowden_bobby01.html

Pooh's Christmas Gifts

To: Alyssa
Merry Christmas

From: Miss Gina

Disney's
Winnie the Pooh First Readers

DISNEP's

A Winnie the Pooh First Reader

Pooh's Christmas Gifts

by Isabel Gaines

ILLUSTRATED BY Mark Marderosian
and Fred Marvin

DISNEP
PRESS

NEW YORK

Pooh's Christmas Gifts

"Tomorrow is Christmas,"

said Kanga.

"And we're having a party!" said Roo.

"So please come to our house

at six o'clock," said Kanga.

"We want to celebrate

with all our friends."

"How fun!" said Pooh.

The next morning

when Pooh woke up,

it was dark outside.

"Oh my," he said.

"It must be six o'clock.

I'm late for the party."

Pooh hurried to Piglet's house.

When he arrived,

Pooh called out,

"Piglet, wake up.

We're late for the party."

Pooh and Piglet woke up

their other friends.

Then they all headed over

to Kanga and Roo's house.

"Merry Christmas!" yelled Pooh.

"Oh dear," said Kanga. "It is six

o'clock in the morning!

I meant six o'clock tonight.

Please come back later,

and then we'll start the party."

Kanga and Roo closed their door.

"What are we going to do

until six o'clock tonight?" asked Pooh.

"Let's make a snowman," said Piglet.

They made three snowballs.

Then they stacked them

one on top of the other.

When they finished,

Tigger said,

"Let's make snow angels!"

They each found a spot

to lie down in the snow,

and then began flapping

their arms, legs, and wings.

Poor Eeyore had trouble

flapping his legs,

so he just rolled around on his back.

They all stood to admire their work.

Everyone's angel was perfect.

Except for Eeyore's.

His angel looked like a blob.

"I need to rest," said Eeyore.

Just then,

Christopher Robin walked by.

"I have a gift for each of you,"

he said.

"Why?" asked Piglet.

"Because on Christmas,

you give gifts

to those you love,"

said Christopher Robin.

21

"We should give

Christopher Robin a gift,"

said Rabbit.

"But what?" asked Tigger.

"I have an idea," said Pooh.

"Christopher Robin," said Pooh,

"we built this snowman.

And we would like

to give it to you

so you're never lonely."

"We made snow angels, too,"

said Piglet.

"We would like you

to have them, as well."

"So you never get lost,"

said Pooh.

"I am sorry mine looks

a little funny," added Eeyore.

25

"Thank you very much,"

said Christopher Robin.

"These are the best kinds of gifts

because they come from the heart."

"Kanga and Roo are giving us

a party," said Rabbit.

"What can we give them?"

asked Tigger.

"I know," said Owl.

"Let's give them a song."

Everyone agreed it was a great idea.

Pooh started the song,

and whenever he got stuck,

somebody would add a word.

Finally, they finished.

They practiced the song

until it was time for the party.

Then they went back

to Kanga and Roo's house,

and knocked on the door.

When Kanga and Roo opened the door,

all of their friends began to sing . . .

"We wish you a Merry Christmas.

We wish you a Merry Christmas.

We wish you a Merry Christmas,

Kanga and Roo.

"It's love that we bring

to share on this day

We wish you a Merry Christmas

with this song—Hurray!"

33

"This is the best gift ever!"

said Kanga. "Please come in

and enjoy the party."

And that's what all the friends did.